This Time
I Will Praise the Lord

THIS TIME
I Will
PRAISE
the LORD

TAYSHA MORALES

XULON PRESS

Xulon Press
2301 Lucien Way #415
Maitland, FL 32751
407.339.4217
www.xulonpress.com

Paperback ISBN-13: 978-1-6628-1990-2
Hard Cover ISBN-13: 978-1-6628-1991-9
Dust Jacket ISBN-13: 978-1-6628-2064-9
eBook ISBN-13: 978-1-6628-1992-6

This book is dedicated to four of the most important men in my life –Eduardo, Tayed, Nathan and Caleb. I don't know what I've done to deserve you all. I'm so fortunate and blessed to be surround by your unwavering love and constant support. Thank you for being a part of this journey with me. For all your words of encouragement and for never allowing me to quit.

You are the best and I love you guys!

Table of Contents

Introduction ix
Acknowledgements xiv

Section I: Lost & Found

Chapter 1   So, What Is Your Story? 1
Chapter 2   Who Am I? 21
Chapter 3   The In Between Process –
                 From Lost To Found 35

Section II: Bounce Back

Chapter 4   I Can, I Will. 59
Chapter 5   There Is No Place Like Home 79
Chapter 6   "Will Thou Be Made Whole?" 101

Conclusion: Birth Your Judah Praise

Chapter 7   The Power and Effect of Praise 127

Appendix A   Scriptures to Discover Your
                 Identity in Christ 159
Appendix B   Scriptures for a Weary Soul 161

About the Author. 163
Endnotes. 165

Introduction

"If at first you don't succeed, try, try again,"
-T. H. Palmer

THE ABOVE PROVERB is traced back to an American educator who used it to encourage schoolchildren to do their homework. If children needed to be encouraged against the deleterious[1] effect of disappointments caused by school assignments, how much more do you think you and I would need to as we journey through life? In life we are bombarded left to right with all kinds of situations that ultimately will require us to decide on how to proceed. It is in moments like that, when caught between a rock and a hard place – feeling the weight of yesterday's failures, the struggles of the present and the uncertainty of tomorrow – we must learn to do as the psalmist stated in Psalm 46:10, "Be still."

Standing still, for most, may seem like a wasted effort. Yet, it's the most satisfying exercise you can do. To be still is not quitting, in fact, it's knowing the God you serve. As you stand "still," you are reminded of who is in control and how everything created, like the floor you are standing on, must submit to His divine power and authority. Let me explain. As your natural eyes sees the concrete floor, your inner man sees the word of God who created the tangible materials that made the floor on which you are standing. Hallelujah!

Therefore, no matter what you may face in life, know that God is in control and you have what it takes to get through it (Philippians 4:13). Don't allow the adversity, discouragement, disappointments, and failures decide that the best thing you can do is quit. Don't give up on your dream, your vision, your marriage, your family, or your assignment. Refuse to settle. I encourage you and pray today, that through this book along with your bible, you find the strength, courage, and guidance needed to endure as you try again. Regardless of what your decision might be – whether to give up or to move forward – know that it will cost you something.

> Your decision will cost you something.

The decision to give up may seem easy and quick, yet the end results will have a lifelong impact on you. Keep in mind that when you give up your days will become burdened with wonders, regrets, and unhappiness. Don't shortchange your future because of the difficulties you are facing today. Embrace it. You are not alone. On the other hand, the cost of going forward is the inability of going back. It's not that you can't go back but going back to what used to be normal will never be the same. Moving forward will demand perseverance, resilience, and determination. Henry Ford stated, "Failure is only the opportunity to begin again, only this time more wisely."[2] Failure doesn't mean it's over, or that it can't be done. The beauty of trying again, is knowing beforehand what did or didn't work. Sadly, we find ourselves falling into the same patterns, repeating the same vicious cycles that quite frankly leaves us in the same situation.

I was told once that life is like a race, it has nothing to do with how fast I could run, rather it's about making it to the finish line. Now, I know that made absolutely no sense whatsoever, as every race has to do with speed, being that only one person takes home the prize. However, life's race has to do with patience, resistance, and stability. These three elements –patience, resistance, and stability – are vitally important and essential to have as we journey through this race. As in any race, there may be obstacles, distractions or detours we didn't anticipate, yet, because we are determined in making it to the finish line, we endure until the end. These obstacles, distractions, or detours can range in magnitude and present themselves in different ways yet serves the same objective – cause you to miss the mark.

When the mark is missed, it is here where we are faced with disappointment and the urge to quit, to give up and go about our way. Yet, it is here, at this precise moment where I would like to encourage you to try again. Yes, rise up, dry your tears, shake off the feeling of failure and give it another try. As Leah, tell your situation, circumstance and self, this time I will do it differently (Genesis 29:35). You may have not had someone to encourage you, but you do now. You have so much to give and offer in this world. A dear friend would always tell me, Taysha, "What is for you is for you and no matter how many challenges you face (which seems like they tend to cause several detours), rest assure that what is for you will always be there. It has been strategically designed and made just for you."

And it is on that note, I sincerely urge you to give whatever has had you down and out, another try. Whether it be your marriage, finances, career, relationships, or even yourself – give it another try. Throughout this book, you'll find biblical principles and real-life stories that will help you to break the cycle and to tell yourself, *I can, and I will*. I can love and I will love. I can forgive and I will forgive. I can do it and I will do it. You'll discover that you can bounce back from anything. Remember, you don't have to do it alone. Turn back to the one who formed you and destined you for greatness. Jeremiah 29:11 says,

"For I know the thoughts that I think toward
you, saith the Lord, thoughts of peace, and not
of evil, to give you an expected end."

Jesus is the source for all of mankind. If we choose to
keep filling our own tank we will stay in the dark, suffering
the pain of loss and despair. Jesus is the light of the world
and He has promised to always be with us, so much so, that
He said until the end of days. Why choose then to live this
life without His guidance? Why attempt to figure out how
to provide for your life when the creator knows what is best
for you? Allow Him the opportunity to do for you what
He intended to do with Adam from the beginning of the
creation, establish a relationship.

A relationship is vital in our life's, whether it be with
God, our spouse, children, family, work, etc. Relationships
are built on communication, trust, and intimacy. You need
to be able to trust the person you're building a relationship
with, while communicating the intimate details of your life.
Our minds tends to carry away when we hear the word intimacy or intimate, however, when I make mention of it, I
refer to such a pure, honest intimacy. Intimacy is exposing
who you truly are without having to feel afraid or ashamed
of anyone judging you. It doesn't matter where you find
yourself right now. Know that God, through His son Jesus,
desires to have a relationship with you. The question you

must honestly answer is whether you are ready to trust Him with your life? Are you willing to exchange your hurts, pains, and failures for His beauty?

If you are that person, I applaud you for taking the first step into your destiny. Know that you were created for purpose and that you have never been a product of the past but a chosen vessel for the Kingdom of God. Embrace your new journey in the Lord and know without a shadow of doubt that he who began the good work in your life shall complete it to its perfection (Philippians 1:6). As you read this book, I pray that God through his Holy Spirit ministers and stirs your life in such a way that by the last page you would have experience a metamorphosis and declare as Leah did, after all her unsuccessful attempts, **"This time I will praise the Lord."**

Acknowledgements:

FIRST AND FOREMOST, I would like to thank my Lord and Savior Jesus Christ for the opportunity granted to be able to share in such way the gospel.

To all my personal editors (you know who you are), thank you for your time, feedback, and support. You guys are awesome!

To my extended family and friends, whom I love and appreciate. Thank you for your continued prayer, support, and encouragement from day one of this writing.

To my home church (Ministerio Pentecostal Nueva Generación (MPNG), thank you, for all your fervent prayers.

To my mother and sisters who believed in me and continued to pray that the Lord would fill me with knowledge, wisdom, and revelation of His word.

Truly yours,
T. Morales

Lost & Found

CHAPTER 1

So, What Is
Your Story?

*At any given moment you have the power to
say, "This is not how my story is going to end." –
Christine Mason Miller*[3]

I'm rewriting my story and it's beautiful.[4] *–
Unknown Author*

EVERYONE HAS A story. Stories define us. Whether
it be long or short, boring or exciting, dramatic or dull,
we all – young and old – have a story to tell. Stories that are
still being written while others are ready to be read and told.

You probably think that no one wants to hear about your story but trust me there is someone out there who needs to hear it, loud and clear. Hear about the ups and downs, the repeated cycles and patterns, the frustrations, failures, seasons of barrenness, and ultimately about the turning point in your life. "Turning points tend to be much more obvious in the telling than in the living."[5] The moment you decided where enough was enough. The moment you took a stand and refused to settle from living beneath your purpose and calling.

I know we much rather speak about the happy moments in life but if truth be told, those happy moments have been predicated upon hard times. The "hard times" aren't meant to keep you down and out, but to help you prepare for the next season in life. We often find that we've become trapped during the season of "hard times," not because we can't get out or rise above, but because we have settled. Most of the time we settle out of fear of pressing forward. In fact, we all have within us a tendency to settle for "less" and a desire for "more." The bible has nothing to say about cowards. The apostle Paul lets us know in 2 Timothy 1:7,

> "For God hath not given us the spirit of fear;
> but of power, and of love, and of a sound mind."

You have the power to choose. Will you settle for less or will you seek to possess all that "rightfully" belongs to you?

In the book of Numbers 27 we find an interesting story of five young ladies –*Mahlah, Noah, Hoglah, Milcah, and Tirzah*—who refused to settle and live under the shadow of fear their father had. They are the daughters of Zelophehad. His name means "dark shadow" or "shadow of fear." He grew up under the shadow of fear in the wilderness as a result of his forefathers, who were terrified to go into the promise land. Remember this? There were twelve spies sent to check out the land and ten returned with a negative report while two –Joshua and Caleb—came back with a positive one (Number 13). When Zelophehad died, the same shadow that hoover around him was now over

SHADOWS DO NOT DIE.

his daughters. Note that SHADOWS DO NOT DIE. A shadow is a dark shape that is formed when an object blocks a source of light.[6]

Shadows are experienced year-round. They tend to be longer during the winter season due to the angle of the sun. Also, the sun makes the longest shadows at the beginning and at the end of the day because at that time, the sun is lowest in the sky and aimed at the sides of the various things on the earth. You will notice that almost every object –living or non-living—will cast a shadow with the exception of glass[7]. Shadows are not harmful nor pose any threats in itself, however, when you give it power it will keep you stuck and afraid in a place that was not made nor is destined for you. The wilderness wasn't a place to live. In fact, the wilderness in the bible was a place designed for intense experiences and served as a platform of preparation before entering into another level in this case, the promise land. Zelophehad's daughter refused to allow the "shadow of fear" gain power over their future. They stood up and brought their request to Moses.

When you know that you were created and destined for more, you don't allow fear to intimidate you. Refuse to settle and know "that all things work together for good to them that love God, to them who are called according to his purpose," according to Romans 8:28. Seasons are inevitable. In nature we cannot have a complete year without going through the four seasons – Spring, Summer, Fall and Winter. During each season, the weather, plants, and animals experience some type of change to prepare them for the next stage to come. What does this mean? Just as we prepare every year for these weather changes, we must adjust and make the necessary changes in our spiritual life during each season. In her book "The Deborah Anointing: Embracing the call to be a woman of wisdom and discernment," Michelle McClain-Walters, describes in depth each season in its spiritually connotation. Take a look below:

- **Spiritual winter Season: a time of death to self**
  Winter is the season with the shortest days, limited sun-
  light, and the lowest average temperatures. It charac-
  teristically has the coldest weather with snow and ice.
  Winter is a time for inclement weather when people
  want to stay inside and hibernate (Matt. 24:20; Mark
  13:18; Acts 27:12; 2 Tim. 4:21 Titus 3:12). Winter is a
  time when you might feel cold and uncomfortable. Any
  farmer will tell you that winter is not a time to plant but
  to begin planning what to plant during the next season.
  Our spiritual winter can seem like a time of darkness,
  as if your life is unfruitful, and you may assume your
  dreams are dying. But during winter there is no fruit
  bearing. It is a time when God kills everything in your
  life that will affect the harvest of the next season in your
  life. Spiritual winter is the most uncomfortable time for
  many Christians. However, this is a season to redefine
  and further develop a relationship with the God of your
  call. This is when God continues to develop your root
  system in Him. There He will give you directions for
  planting new crops in spring, which is the next season.
  Spiritual winter is the time for evaluation, planning,
  and preparation. It is a time for letting go of anything
  that will destroy your call. It is also the time to learn
  the uniqueness of your call. In this season God will
  begin to enlighten the eyes of your understanding (Eph.

5

1:18). He may give you a calling, assignment, dream, or promise, and you many have no understanding of what it is or how it is supposed to function or be accomplished. You may wonder why God chose you for this calling. You may look around at the ability of others and wonder why God did not call them instead of you. During spiritual winter it is normal to feel as if everyone else seems to be better qualified and better equipped. At this same time, you are also wondering why you feel so compelled toward a particular are of ministry or service. This dilemma stirs a desire to seek God about the call on your life. You may feel as if you are having a "wilderness" experience –as if God is not hearing your prayers or speaking to you. I have heard it taught that the wilderness is a place of God's punishment. I believe that the wilderness is where you finally meet God. Hosea 2:14 gives us a different picture of the wilderness:

> Therefore, I will allure her, and bring her into
> the wilderness, and speak tenderly to her.

The wilderness is the place you begin to see yourself in the light of His glory. It's where you encounter God and kill the beast of your soul that would hinder the call of God. The wilderness is the place where you die to self. the inclination is to pray harder or more, but you must remain in the season of rest. Spiritual winter is a time of reflection and meditation. It is a season of questions and answers between you and the Holy Spirit for the details of your life. It's a time of measurement. As questions begin to arise in your heart, you may ask the Lord:

- Who are you, Lord? The answer to that question also reveals who you are.

- What do you want me to do? The answer to that question is the opening of clarification and direction for His call on your life.

- **Spiritual spring: a time to embrace the call**
  Spring marks the transition from winter into summer. According to the Bible, Spring is the time when kings go off to war (See 2 Samuel 11:1; 1 Chronicles 20:1.). Maybe this is why Deborah knew it was time for Israel to go to war. Springtime is also the rainy season. God aided Deborah and Barak by causing torrential rains to fall from the sky, causing Sisera and his men with nine hundred chariots to be stuck in the mud, causing them to be inoperable. Spring is the time for romance with descriptions of buds and blossoms (Songs 2:11-14; 7:11-13). Spring brings new leaves and blossoms on the trees. In the spiritual realm spring is the time to plant

and carry out the instructions gleaned from your winter experience. You will begin to implement the instructions you've gained from spending time with God in the wilderness. Because you've rested and encountered God in the wilderness, you will have fresh, new revelation of God. This newfound revelation will empower you with spiritual and physical energy to break up your fallow ground.

This expression, "Break up your fallow ground" (Hos. 10:12; Jer. 4:3) means, "Do not sow your seed among thorns," i.e., break off all your evil habits. Clear your hearts of weeds, in order that they may be prepared for the seed of righteousness. Land was allowed to lie fallow that it might become more fruitful, but when in this condition, it soon became overgrown with thorns and weeds. The cultivator of the soil was careful to "break up" his fallow ground, i.e., to clear the field of weeds, before sowing seed in it. So says the prophets, "Break off your evil ways, repent of your sins, cease to do evil, and then the good seed of the word will have room to grow and bear fruit."

Ask yourself, in what ways have I been stagnant or neutral about pursuing the purpose of God for my life? What is required of me to change this position of stagnation and neutrality? In the spring season begin to develop a new confidence in the God of your calling. There is newfound faith in God's ability to accomplish His calling through you. There is new desire to be equipped and trained in the calling. There is a new aligning of your heart for your assignment, a new desire for deliverance to remove anything that would hinder the call. God will send you new connections, mentors, and relationships to help fulfill the call. Desire to discover the full depth of your calling, assignment, or dream.

- **Spiritual summer: a time of revelation**
  Summer is the time to water what has been planted during the spring. Summer is the most dangerous season because of the heat (natural and spiritual). Summer is a time of both growth and of stillness, of hard work in the fields and of relaxing in the cool of the day. Summer is a time for both work and play. This is where you learn to balance your natural life and spiritual calling. This is a time of wisdom and revelation. There will even be opportunity to minister in some level of the call and anointing on your life. Everything seems to come to life after a long Winter and Spring. In this Summer season you come to know and understand some of the depths, requirements, and specifics of the call. The initial fear and anxiety calmed down, and

you will become confident in accepting the call of God. You will say, "For I know whom I have believed, and am persuaded..." (2 Tim. 1:12). Paul moved from not knowing God to wanting to know God, and then his desires was fulfilled as he began to relate to the God of the call. You will know God in increasing levels of relational intimacy through worship, prayer, and the Word. You will become confident of what God has called you to do – His purpose. You will be persuaded that the God of the call is able to make sure that His calling is fulfilled in your life. Ask yourself, how am I growing in my relations with Jesus? How would I describe my level of confidence in my assignment?

- **Spiritual fall: a time of harvest and fulfillment**
  Provided you have been diligent during the previous seasons, Fall is the time of harvest. Fall is the time when you will see evidence of your hard work. It is a time of harvesting and storing up for the winter. This is the season filled with anticipation. And if we have been obedient in the other seasons, we will reap a harvest in due season (Gal. 6:9). Autumn is a season of fruition and reaping. It is a season of thanksgiving and celebration of the abundance and goodness of the earth. In this season you are living with the assurance that the instructions assigned to you in the call of God have

been fulfilled or carved out to their fullest expression. This assurance produces a desire for a reward. You realize that there is a reward for those who complete God's assignment according to His blueprint for their lives. You will realize that you have finished your course or your assignment. You will also realize that you have kept the faith or remained in courage and trust in God and His ability to fulfill everything He has declared for your life. You will submit yourself to the price or sacrificial demands of God's call, and from that posture of humility you will evoke a response from God, receiving your reward.

> But without faith it is impossible to please and be satisfactory to Him. For whoever would come near to God must [necessarily] believe that God exists and that He is the rewarder of those who earnestly and diligently seek Him [out]. – Hebrews 11:6, AMP

At this season it is important that you believe that God is actively engaged in every detail of your life and that He will reward you if you are continually pursuing Him. God has a call for your life, but you must be ready and willing to act according to His times and seasons. As you move forward in your God-given destiny, persevering, capitalizing, and maximizing every season, you will develop the capacity to walk as a modern-day Deborah in the earth. You will be like Deborah the Issacharite, discerning the time and seasons of your life and gaining wisdom on what to do[8].

As we live through the gift of life, we must embrace each season and be ready for what comes next. I know this sounds challenging. The thought to embrace a season without knowing for sure what to expect but know that "to everything there is a season, and a time to every purpose under the heaven," according to Ecclesiastes 3:1. It's such an opportunity to come to know God on another level. Abraham, after waiting years for the fulfillment of a promise, God, tells him to offer up his son as a sacrifice. What? Yes, the same God who promised him a son, gave him a son, now asks him for the son. Here, during this season, Abraham experienced God as Jehovah Jireh – *my provider (Genesis 22)*. During what season do you find yourself right now? Are you willing to trust God? If not, are you able to identify what is hindering your ability to trust God in the season you are in?

Now many years later, we find that as Jesus was getting ready to depart this earth, he prepared his disciples for the next season in their life. In the book of John, we find that he told them that in this world they would have many afflictions. Furthermore, that he would give them something that although the world offered it, it wasn't quite the same. Peace. He gave them peace. He proceeded to tell them not to allow their hearts to be consumed with trouble or fear. See for every season in life we are provided with the peace and comfort we'll need to go through until the next one. It is our job not to allow the changes, circumstances, afflictions of that season to inundate our hearts with troubles or fear. If we allow fear to take place and control our hearts, we will then be paralyzed, unable to move forward. Fear is the opposite of faith. Where faith pushes you to walk, fear paralyzes and immobilizes you from seizing the moment at hand.

Moments don't usually announce themselves. They just happen. A "moment" can change it all. Don't let your fears make you miss your moment. Don't let your failures, frustrations, and your present situation stop you from the moment you've been waiting for. Instead, brace yourself this day with the peace Jesus has left you. His peace provides rest and rejuvenates our soul as we move through the constant changes and cycles of life. Peace is the assurance or guarantee that there is a light at the end of the tunnel. His peace passes all understanding and can keep our hearts and mind according

> A "moment" can change it all.

to Philippians 4:7. Let's be bold enough together to tell the pieces of our stories we would like to hit a delete button and erase forever. See, it's those little things that helps others know that this too shall pass. That if you were able to overcome, survive and keep moving, they too can do so.

The psalmist didn't praise God because someone taught him to or because he saw his parents and siblings do so. He praised God because of the things he went through that only God could help him survive through. One of my favorite verses found in the Bible is that of David in Psalms 34:1,

> "I will bless the Lord at all times, his praise shall continually be on my lips."

Regardless of being persecuted, hated, and hunted, he knew that he owed an offering of praise to the Lord for his goodness and mercy. It was God who helped him in his life even when he spent half his time running in the wilderness, hiding from cave to cave from the one man who he valued and esteemed. He didn't understand the whys, but he knew that despite not understanding, God needed to be praised. He was committed to giving God the one thing he could give Him – Praise.

Allow me a moment to interject something here. I'm not talking about a sweet melodic[9] sound of praise. One that we can shout or harmonize beautifully in church while singing. I'm talking about a radical, nonsense praise. One that makes you lose your mind, forget who you are and where you are. A praise that shifts' you from Earth to Heaven without leaving that room or place. Until you've been through some valleys, you won't understand David's praise. His praise took him to take off his robe and dance before the Lord, while his wife, Michal, belittled and despised him as she looked through the window (2 Samuel 6:16). David did not allow his position to hold him back from giving God his praise. He couldn't afford not to praise God. Therefore, he didn't allow his failures, past sins, belittlement of his wife, and position as King to stop him from praising. Have you allowed your story to stop you from praising God? Know today that your praise has power to transcend the atmosphere like a sphere and give you the breakthrough needed.

> Your praise has power to transcend the atmosphere like a sphere.

Provided below is a glimpse of the story behind the praise of these women:

- **Leah**: Her true and genuine praise was birthed from experiencing God as a way maker. Her praise came from a place of pain. Yes, pain. The pain of rejection, loneliness, and hatred. She was given unto marriage by her father, Laban, to a man he knew was head over heels for his other daughter, Rachel. Leah, despite knowing that she was entering into a deceptive marriage, she longed that eventually her husband would grow to love her. After so many unsuccessful attempts in finding happiness, joy, fulfillment, satisfaction, approval, meaning, value, purpose, and connection she boldly declares, "This time I will praise the Lord." She took hold of that which had held her hostage for so many years and turned her story around. She had one of the most amazing encountered with God in the midst of her situation. Although there is no record found in scriptures that her present situation may have changed, we do find that she was not the same woman thereafter.

- **Hannah**: Her praise is produced out of bareness and bitterness. Her bareness wasn't physical but spiritual. According to scriptures her womb was shut up by God. What? Yes, God had not allowed Hannah to produce a child yet. Hannah's husband Elkanah had another wife called Peninnah. Peninnah had no issues giving her husband children. In fact, every year she would remind Hannah of how fruitful she was with Elkanah. This would provoke Hannah to become irritated, sad, and angry. So much that every year when it was time to go up to Shiloh and present their sacrifice, Hannah would become irritated. Hannah was in a dry and barren season. Oftentimes, we as Hannah cannot see beyond what we are living in the moment. And it is in this season that God remembered Hannah.

- **Bent over Women**: Her praise was produced out of being marginalized for eighteen years. Luke is the only writer who speaks about this woman in the gospel. He states that this woman spent eighteen years of her life bent over. Imagine for a quick moment what your life would be or look like if this was you? Not a pretty scene, right? In this story, we see how Jesus heals, delivers, and restores this woman who had been bound by the enemy. Although Luke doesn't provide what the woman had done to end up like this for eighteen years, he does share that there is nothing our almighty God can't do to bring us back to where we belong. That's the power of restoration.

- **Samaritan Women**: This is the first woman to evangelize in the world. You would have thought that in order to carry out such task one must have been raised in church, graduated from seminary school and commissioned to go forth, and of course a male. Yet, in God's plan and design He chooses a woman and not just an ordinary woman. This woman was well known in

Samaria. She had been with five different man according to Jesus and the one she was shacking up with was not her husband. After a conversation with Jesus, she let go of her water pot and went into the city to testify about the encounter she had had with Jesus. Her praise was produced out of the truth she confessed during her conversation with Jesus, which made her free. No more living in shame.

- **Rahab**: From the whorehouse to the royal lineage. Talk about a story. Her praise is produced from the mercy shown to her by God. Mercy, at its core definition, is no other than forgiveness. Rahab along with her people from Jericho was on the list to perish. However, she received compassion, love, and forgiveness. Her act of kindness towards the man who entered to spy the land ended up in saving her life and those who were in her home. Thank goodness that God's mercy doesn't discriminate, that it isn't afraid to go to the lowest places of life to save and rescue those that do not deserve it. Rahab experienced firsthand, what God told Moses in Exodus 33:19, "And will be gracious to whom I will be gracious and will shew mercy on whom I will shew mercy."

- **<u>You and I</u>**: Our stories are no different than the ones above. We all have experienced good and bad times that we wouldn't mind sharing. Now, we also have those moments in life that if truth be told we are ashamed of. We wish there was a way to erase it as if it never happened. But I've come to learn and accept my darkest past as part of the reason of my existence.

"To change our stories, we need to engage with them, to dialogue with then and to gently, consistently and persistently change the way the narrative goes"[10]. With that said, if you had discounted yourself because of all the ups and downs, repeated cycles and failures experienced in your life, I urge you this day and moment to give it another try. Pick up the pencil, pass the page and begin writing a new chapter in your life. Don't worry about yesterday, God has that. Focus on what's at hand today, as tomorrow will take care of itself (Matthew 6:34). Remember, nobody can tell your story like you. Therefore, seize each and every opportunity given to share with others the story behind your praise. **How will your story end?**

> Nobody can tell your story like you.

CHAPTER 2

Who Am I?

For we are his workmanship, created in Christ Jesus unto good works, which God hath before ordained that we should walk in them.
Ephesians 2:10

D O YOU KNOW who you are? This is one of the most difficult, yet simple question to answer in life – *"Who am I?"* The question does not seek to only know your name or background, although these are important factors, it seeks to know what makes you, you. I don't know about you, but I have asked myself this question so many

21

times that I've lost count. And if I was to be honest with you, I still do. The only difference now is that the question doesn't originate from where it did at first. See, most of us ask the question from a comparative standpoint of view. Comparison? Yes, we all do it, even though we know it's not right. When we compare our self to others, we lose sight of who we are and our true value. We see this in the story of Leah and Rachel found in Genesis 29. In this passage, the writer provides a few details that most of us may deem insignificant. Yet, I've learned, that it is in the smallest and insignificant details where the true message and pertinent information lies.

The writer lets you know that Leah was the first-born and Rachel the younger child. And then he takes the time to describe them in Genesis 29:17,

> "Leah was *tender eyed*; but Rachel was *beautiful and well favoured*" (emphasis added).

It is here, where I allude that Leah lost sight of who she was. All was going well with her, until the day Rachel, her sister, joined the family. You see, as long as there is no one close enough with whom we can compare ourselves to, we are A-OK with whatever our —weaknesses, defects, family problems, marital issues, cycles, secrets, addictions and so forth – may be. However, when you look around and everything you see reminds you of your failures, your inabilities, or your limitations, you tend to lose yourself within. When you are lost within your own self, your vision becomes distorted about who you are and what your purpose in life is. In Matthew 6:22-23, we are told that,

> "The light of the body is the eye: if therefore thine eye be single, thy whole body shall be full of light. But if thine eye be evil, thy whole body shall be full of darkness. If therefore the light that is in thee be darkness, how great is that darkness!"

Both Leah and Rachel had no control whatsoever over what their outer appearance would look like. Just like you and I don't' have that control, it is simply something beyond us. Can you imagine for a second if we did have that control over what we would look like when born into this world? What would the world around us look like? Would it be different than what it is today? If so, what would be different? Leah allowed herself to place the value of her existence on the outer man rather than the inner man. It's so easy to lose sight of who we are when someone who is perhaps more eloquent, more favorable, more talented, or more prepared than us appears.

It is why our eyes should stay centered on Jesus, "The author and finisher of our faith" Hebrews 12:2. Peter allowed the boisterous[11] wind to cause him to lose sight of the one who bid him to "come" and walk on water (Matthew 14:22-33). We all have gone through this cycle once or twice (maybe more) in life. We find that those who are tall compare themselves with those who are average or shorter, while you have those who are blonde or brunet comparing themselves with those who are not. Therefore, attempting to answer the question "Who am I?" by what is seen in the outside, can cause us to miss God's grandeur masterpiece.

A masterpiece is a work of outstanding artistry, skill, or workmanship. If you don't get anything else from this book or this chapter alone, let the following truth about who you are permeate the depth of your soul. You are not only the product of the union and love of your parents, you are God's MASTERPIECE. You are not a mistake. You are not here by accident. You are here because you are the

> You are here because you are the intention of the thought from God's heart.

intention of the thought from God's heart. God's intention with you didn't begin the day you were born. It began when he said in Genesis 1:26, let us make man according to our image and after our likeness. You were planned, purposed, and planted into this world for such a time as this. I don't know about you, but this causes for a *Selah*[1] moment.

Leah may have felt and saw herself as the ugly duckling, inferior to those around her due to what she saw in the mirror, yet when God saw her, he saw a magnificent, extraordinary, and beautiful masterpiece. He saw the woman who would become the mother of seven[12] out of the twelve children of Jacob, who later would form the tribes of Israel. Have you ever taken the time to know how God sees you and what he has to say about you? Or are you more interested in what others see or have to say about you than what God does? God's view of you has nothing to do with how you or others think or feel about you. His thoughts are far above yours according to Isaiah 55:8-9. To help you understand this, below you'll find how God saw them in spite of what they thought of themselves and what others had to say or think about them:

- Abraham: Father of Faith & Friend of God (James 2:23)
- Moses: Deliverer (Exodus 3)
- Joshua: Strong and Courageous (Joshua 1:6,7,9)
- Gedeon: Mighty Warrior (Judges 6:12)

---

[1] **Selah:** an expression occurring frequently in the Psalms, thought to be liturgical or musical direction, probably a direction by the leader to raise the voice or perhaps an indication of a pause.

- David: Man, after God's heart
- Jeremiah: Prophet (Jeremiah 1:5)
- Mary: Highly favored (Luke 1:28)
- Bent over woman: Daughter of Abraham (Luke 13:16)

When our focus is placed on the outer appearance, we will eventually devalue who we are. Think about it for a minute, how many years did Leah waste in the famous "comparing cycle" game? Did she gain anything beneficial to her exterior appearance? Absolutely not. In fact, she was left lost and weary. We will discuss this further in the next chapter. Leah was far too lost within herself to realize what God had done on her behalf (Genesis 29:31). As she longed for what Rachel had –beauty, connection, and love– Rachel wanted what Leah had – the privilege to bear children.

As Leah, we find today many people – woman, men, young, old – who struggles with acceptance, lack of self-esteem, rejection, abandonment issues, and the list just go on. When we are not able to see our value, we compromise the reason of our existence. You were created on purpose for a purpose. Everything about you, has been designed by God to serve His purpose. You would think that as God's masterpiece, we would be content with His

> You were created on purpose for a purpose.

final display, yet we find that most of us are not. Look at what the apostle Paul had to say in Romans 9:20 (NIV):

> "But who are you, a human being, to talk back to God?" Shall what is formed say to the one who formed it, "Why did you make me like this?"

The prophet Jeremiah shares a vivid portrait of his experience at the potters' house in Jeremiah 18. Little did he know that he would be witnessing one of the most intimate moments the potter has with the clay during its process in the making. When he arrived at the potter's house, he was captivated by the potters' hands, the constant spinning wheel and the clay during its' formation stages – before, during and after. As Jeremiah patiently waited to hear from the Lord, I could only imagine the thoughts and questions that crossed his mind as he "*beheld*" the scene that was unfolding right before him. He was intrigued by how the potter exhibited full control over both the wheel and the clay. The potter was able to synchronize his feet and hands to one accord as the thought and plan he envisioned was being formed in the clay. To Jeremiah's surprise (and mine) the vessel he had so patiently been working with was marred. The interesting detail in the passage is that the vessel was marred in the hands of the potter. I can understand becoming marred in the hands of someone else, but not in the hands of the potter. But what took Jeremiah's breath away, was what the potter did next. He took the same clay who had been "damaged" in the process and began to work with it again, making it a new vessel as he saw fit. The potter didn't quit on the clay. He didn't walk out or away from it. Why then do we as the clay, give up on God?

It was customary to discard that which was useless. Every potter at the end of the day was left with one or two vessels that in the process had become marred and needed to be thrown away. In addition, it was also customary for the potter to show a certain degree of annoyance when seeing his work unfulfilled. Yet, on this day, Jeremiah saw quite the opposite. Not only did the potter pick up the now "damaged" clay, He continued to show the same affection – compassion, patience and love – as he did when he first started working with it. Mind blowing, huh? Jeremiah soon realized that this is what the prophet Isaiah meant when he wrote in Isaiah 64:8:

> "But now, O Lord, thou art our father; we are
> the clay, and thou our potter; and we all are the
> work of thy hand."

This was the message the Lord was going to "cause" Jeremiah to hear. God as the potter does not have to put up with the clay's refusal to take form or shape. He can easily get rid of it and start the process again with another lump of clay.

This is what he told Moses in Deuteronomy 9:12-14, when His people had provoked Him over and over again by choosing to alter the purpose of their existence. However, with God there is always the opportunity to become what He originally intended in spite of ourselves, to still be properly shaped to His purpose. Do you know how many people were marred in the hands of the potter (God) and yet by His sovereignty became what He intended? Look at the following list:

- *Adam & Eve*: The first couple to be created by God. He was known to meet with God daily in the Garden of Eden, but one day he did what he was not supposed to and opened the door to sin, and it hasn't been quite the same since, however *God still had a plan...* (Genesis 1 – 4)

- *Aaron*: Chosen by God to serve his brother Moses as a mouthpiece, yet he allowed himself to be persuaded by the people to build a golden calf to worship as Moses was taking too long up on the mountain with God. And yet we find that *God still had a plan* with Aaron and his children (Exodus 4:15-16; 28:1-2; 32:1-6).

- **David**: The man after the heart of God who was chosen, anointed, and appointed to be the next king of Israel, yet failed countlessly before the Lord, but knew the power of humiliation. And yet we find that **God still had a plan** (2 Samuel 11-12; 2 Samuel 24).

- **Jonah**: Given a message as God's mouthpiece, yet he chose to flee in the opposite direction. And yet we find that **God had a plan** (Jonah 1 – 4).

- **Peter**: Went from being handpicked to walk with Jesus, to walking on waters (even if it was for a second) to denying Jesus as he was arrested and heading to be crucified. And yet **God still had a plan** (Matthew 4:18; 14:30; 26:75).

- **Paul**: Also known as Saul, Paul was one of the early church persecutors. He was neither afraid nor showed any remorse for torture and killing those who believed in Jesus Christ. And yet **God still had a plan** (Acts 8 – 9; Galatians 1:15-17).

- **Naomi**: Moved with her family in a time of famine from Bethlehem to the camps of Moab. Unbeknownst to her, she loses her husband and two sons and to top it all off became bitter in the process. And yet we find that ***God still had a plan*** (Ruth 1 – 4).

Each and every of the names mentioned above and many more like them, became marred in the hands of the potter. However, God still had a plan. A well thought out plan that covered our end from its beginning. A plan that accounted for all the mishaps, the ups and downs and failures that we would go through in life. He knew what you were capable of doing before he started to form you. This is why he chooses not to quit on you as you travail those rough patches in life that cause you to miss the mark. He doesn't walk out when you become frustrated or gives up when you fall back into your same old habits. He remains in the same position, in fact so much closer than we can imagine. When God called Jeremiah, He told him in Jeremiah 1:5 (NIV, emphasis added),

> "Before I formed you in the womb, I knew you. Before you were born, I set you apart. I appointed you as a prophet to the nations."

I want you to take note of this, before God telling Jeremiah what his purpose or mission would be, he told him "Before I formed thee, I knew you." The same is with you and I, God knew us and still knows us and will always know us. He knew you before you had a form or name. He knew you before and after the divorce, or before and after that thing that messed you up. He knew you and because of that there isn't anything about you that he doesn't already know that can cause him not to fulfill his plan and purpose.

Therefore, the million-dollar question "Who am I?" should be asked as a rhetorical question rather than a wondering question. When you know who you are in God your outer shortcomings will be greatly compensated in your inner man. Knowing who you are is winning half the battle. The other half is standing strong and firm in the confidence of who you are and to whom you belong. You and I carry our own set of uniqueness (virtues, qualities and traits given by God) that sets us apart and we must learn to celebrate that as the psalmist did in Psalms 139. Instead of crying and feeling sad for his shortcomings or deficiencies, he chose to praise God for the marvelous work He had done with him. We spend too much time looking at what we don't have – height, shape, length, economic status, education, ministry, talents, etc. – instead of what we do. Take a look at what the apostle Paul said in 2 Corinthians 4:7-9,

> "But we have this treasure in jars of clay to show
> that this all-surpassing power is from God and
> not from us. We are hard pressed on every side,

but not crushed; perplexed, but not in despair; persecuted, but not abandoned; struck down, but not destroyed."

Are you familiar with this quote, "Mirror, mirror on the wall who's the fairest of them all?" In the movie Snow White and the Seven Dwarfs, the evil Queen who was vain, would constantly go to the mirror seeking to know who was the fairest of all. Time after time she longed for the mirrors' response to be "You, Oh, my Queen, are the fairest of them all," yet as expected, the mirror never lied. You've watched the movie and you can confirm that the mirror

> A mirror will never lie.

indeed was not lying, right? A mirror will never lie. No matter where you buy it, or how big or small you buy it and even the amount of money you pay for it – the mirror will not lie.

Mirrors serve many different purposes. However, one of its main tasks is to reverse the direction of the image in equal yet opposite angle from which the light shines upon. In other words, you come face to face with yourself with the help of a mirror. As you journey to find the response to the question "Who am I?" I invite you to take a look in the mirror called The Bible. This mirror will not lie. Its truth has the power to set you free according to John 8:32.

When God gave Moses the blueprints for the construction of the tabernacle, He was specific and very adamant with the instructions given. In all that Moses was given to do, one of the pieces of furniture – *The Bronze Laver*— was made from the mirrors donated by the women (Exodus 38:8 NIV). As the priest enter the tabernacle, before they could serve in their function, they needed to wash both their hands and feet at the laver. The laver had a twofold purpose. It first gives you a reflection of what you look like – before and after. Secondly, it cleanses you.

Just as what The Bible is for us, a mirror, the laver was for the priest – a constant reminder of who they were and to whom they belong. So, if you've lost sight of who you are and to whom you belong, take a stroll down to the bronze laver. There will be no mistake about who you are in Him. You are who He says you are. There is no if and but's about it. Know that in Christ we don't need to depend on our beauty, talents, ability, or others. Instead, we must know our place and position in Him and it's a wrap from there. That alone deserves a praise. *Praise Break!*

> There will be no mistake about who you are in Him. You are who He says you are.

CHAPTER 3

The In Between Process – From Lost To Found

Not until we are lost do we begin to understand ourselves.[13] *– Henry David Thoreau*

ALL MY LIFE I've lived in the same state, same city, and on the same side of town, except for five years, when I lived in Puerto Rico. As a kid, there were things I didn't pay attention to while in a car like the one doing the driving had to do. I simply sat back and enjoyed the ride, asking some of the most annoying questions drivers could be asked. Are we there yet? How much longer? Also, getting lost as a kid really didn't worry me as much as it did when I was older and now doing the driving. When you've lived in the same state and city for a long time, you tend to become familiar with all the different places around you. At least, that's what I thought. Little did I know when I began to drive, I found that the city I lived in was bigger than I thought. So big that if not careful, the slightest distraction could leave you lost.

When I married my husband, I had barely started to drive. At that time, we only had one vehicle. Therefore, there were days when I would drop him off at work to stay with the car in order to do some errands. He had shown me the route I needed to take to and from his job. I had followed this route several times with no trouble. Until one day. This day started like any other day. I drove my husband to work, kissed, and wished him a blessed day and headed back home. Well, so I thought! The road I once was familiar and comfortable with now looked different, unfamiliar, and scary. If you've ever been lost, you know that the least thing you feel is ease, tranquility, and peace. Instead, it's like a gigantic blanket that covers you from head to toe in fear, panic, and anxiety, leaving you vulnerable and exposed to whatever may lay ahead.

King Solomon sheds some insight about roads and its destinations in the book of Proverbs 14:25:

"There is a way which seemeth right unto a man,
but the end thereof are the ways of death."

Although roads may look alike and serve the same purpose, the destination will not be the same. Not all roads will connect you to your destiny. Apparently, I had missed my exit only to find myself in an unfamiliar place. In the era we live in, it's so much easier to get lost, than what it is to be found. Surrounded by many different types of distractions, if you're not careful, we may find that we have detoured off the road that leads us to our destiny. If there is one thing you can always count on that will never fail, are the numerous distractions you'll face on the road.

Distractions can disguise themselves as what they are not. They can also range in various of ways. We find in scriptures several stories of people who slightly missed the moment because of distractions. One of my favorites is that of Martha. Martha was distracted from having an intimate moment, like Mary, with Jesus by a simple, daily, and ordinary house chore. The daily house chores distracted her from the moment that she may had been waiting for her whole life. Despite the reason that led me to where I was, lost in an unfamiliar place, I knew I had a choice to make. A choice to either give up and remain lost or a choice to be found. Choice is defined as the right, power, or opportunity to choose.

See, no situation, adversity or person can force you to do something you don't want to do. We choose between that which is set before us. The road could not force me to say in the unfamiliar place. The unfamiliar place could not force me to allow my feelings to dictate my future. Feelings are fickle. They come and go and will change as quickly as a heartbeat. Although feelings are real, you must be vigilant as they can lead you to believe things that are not true about yourself and others. For instance, you probably feel alone in this world, but the matter of the fact is that you are not alone (Psalm 27:10, 91; John 14:18). You probably feel unloved, but the truth of the matter is that you are loved (John 3:16; 1 John 3:1). You probably feel that you are a failure who won't mount up to anything, but the truth is that you are more than an overcomer (Romans 8:37). Nevertheless, at the end of the day you are left with an opportunity to change your situation by the power of a choice not a feeling. Therefore, don't negotiate your future and destiny based on the feelings your'e experiencing today. What will your choice be? Have you weight in your options? How will your choice affect you not only now but the next five to ten years of your life?

For me, I made a sound choice between my options – lost or found. My choice led me to pull over, make a phone call, receive instructions and ultimately arriving home. When I pulled over and made the phone call, I was so relieved to hear the voice on the other side. My husband asked me two questions. One I couldn't answer because I didn't know or recognize the place I was at. It was an unfamiliar scenery. But I was able to answer the other one. Although everything was unfamiliar, I was able to retract my steps to know if I had taken a wrong turn or not. I had missed my exit and the road once familiar, turned in to an unfamiliar place just minutes away from my destination – home. Can you believe it? Lost within my own vicinity.

Because my choice was to be found, it was vitally important that I followed the instructions being given on the other side of the phone. My husband who had no clue where I was, working only with the information I provided, said that the only thing I needed to do was to turn around and follow the signs back home. What? You mean to tell me that a turn will position me back on the road that leads to my destination. Yes, as simple as that. Guess what I did? I followed the instructions. I trusted that voice of confidence, that although he wasn't physically present with me, he knew how to disarm and de-authorize the power of fear over my life, in order to get me back on the road. Fear's objective is to paralyze you wherever you are at. Fear doesn't respect nor cares about age, gender, status quo, etc., its mission is to stop you from trying each time you fail in life.

Now, it's one thing to be physically lost, like in another city, town, country, parking lot, grocery store, and so forth. But what happens when you are lost within your own self, your own skin, your own element? I bet you never thought of that. Go ahead, have a "Selah" moment. You probably thought that could never happen. However, if truth would be told, many of us have experienced this type of lost just as Leah did. Leah somehow and somewhere became distracted that she ended up lost in the shadow of her sister, Rachel. What has you distracted today?

> It's one thing to be physically lost, like in another city, town, country, parking lot, grocery store, and so forth. But what happens when you are lost within your own self, your own skin, your own element?

As mentioned in previous chapter, Leah was left not only lost but weary. Her name in Hebrew is translated to "weary." Have you ever been exhausted? Not just simply saying you're tired or exhausted. But exhausted at trying to work hard on your marriage, your finances, work, interpersonal relationships, and at the end of the day the results are not what you expected? Have you ever tried so desperately to seek someone's attention and approval (without thinking of the consequences it may have) and yet, you remain unnoticed? Have you ever thought that the world might be a better place without you in it? I believe we've all have had moments in our lives where we have gone to extreme measures in an attempt to alleviate the ache felt in our hearts when there's a void. Although The Bible does not have much to say about Leah, we are able to connect in more ways than one with her life, if truth be told. Leah who had spent her early years comparing herself with Rachel, due to what she lacked externally, she now finds herself in a marriage where she seems not to catch a break.

In a nutshell, she is married to a man by the name Jacob, who had worked seven years for her sister, Rachel. And on the wedding day, instead of Rachel going home with Jacob, Leah did. Not by choice. According to Laban, the custom of the land was that the youngest couldn't be given unto marriage until the oldest was married. Whether or not Leah liked the idea of being given to a man who she knew neither loved nor wanted her, she went along with her father's wicked plan. Perhaps Leah envisioned this moment as her opportunity to freedom from the silent hell she'd had been living. However, not even twenty-four hours into her new life as Mrs. Jacob's, she's hit with a double whammy. After consummating their nuptial all night long, she awakens by an awful stare on the face of the man she hoped would love her as much as she knew he loved Rachel. She then learns that the one she had fled from would now be given to Jacob as a second wife in just a couple of days. As if it wasn't enough living in the shadow of Rachel, she's now married to a man who looks at her but doesn't see her, who listens to her but doesn't hear her, who joins with her but is not united with her.

How many people you and I know of who enters into all sorts of relationships attempting to escape the so-called hell they think they are living in not realizing that they are entering Hell itself? Getting a new boyfriend or girlfriend, or a different spouse won't solve your issues. Buying a new car, or a new home or getting a new haircut or wardrobe may soothe your ache momentarily, but it definitely will not fill the void in your heart. What you don't confront you won't overcome

> What you don't confront you won't overcome and in order to overcome you must be willing to identify the underlying issue.

and in order to overcome you must be willing to identify the underlying issue. The problem in not confronting the issue will leave you drained, both mentally and physically. This is where we must be vigilant as to not allow weariness to enter and arrest us at bay.

There are two types of weariness. One we experience as a result of doing the Lord's work, in which Isaiah 40:30 guarantees renewal of strength. On the other hand, there is an unhealthy type of weariness that strives in the power of the flesh. It is the result of misguided motives[14]. Weariness comes in different shapes and sizes, and its main objective is to destroy any connection to the source of your existence – God. Leah had been working overtime as she was trying to gain her husband's love, affection, and attention. We are painted a picture of what her heart ache looked like through her first three pregnancies in Genesis 29:31-34. She longed to be seen, heard and to be united. Yet, with each pregnancy, the lack thereof continued to sap her energy leaving her depleted. Often, we find ourselves just like Leah, at trying to gain from men (both men and women) that which only can come from God.

> There is nobody on Earth, that will see us, hear us and unite with us like our God.

Let me explain. There is nobody on Earth, that will see us, hear us and unite with us like our God. God, who

43

strategically designed you. Therefore, He understands you and knows exactly what you need and when you need it. The writer of the book of Luke, shares a unique and fascinating story, one that I'm sure you've heard many times before. She's known as the bent over woman. This woman had been living like this for the past eighteen years. Think about that, eighteen years. I'm quite sure that she must had visited several physicians in her days to deal with the condition she was facing. How many physicians do you think this woman saw? And yet, after each touch from the hands of the physician(s), she remained in the same condition, *bent over*. How about home remedies? I'm sure she knew some of those people who have a quick remedy for everything. They are the ones who sound a little like this, well if you take this and do this then you will see this. But you have to do it like this for this amount of time for it to work. Sounds familiar? Yet, after trying the home remedies, she's left quite the same. Nothing seemed to work for her through those eighteen years. Do you think she tried all she could? Did all she could? What would you have done or what else would you have tried if you were in her shoes? As if, she was left with a new "normal" she had to get used to.

But what I find compelling in Luke 13, as her story unfolds is that although nothing had seemed to work for her "yet," she was at the synagogue. The same place she had been going to for the last eighteen years would become the place where she'd experience that inexplicable moment. This is why perseverance is vital for what comes next. We all face uncertainties, afflictions, difficulties, but not all are willing to persevere in the face of. The cost to persevere is too high, that we rather settle with the new "normal." Her perseverance paid off creating a moment within time just for her. A moment that although did not announce itself, the moment changed it all for her. As you continue to read this passage, it was Jesus who called her out and not the other way around. You would have thought that she would be the one pressing through the crowd as the woman of the issue of blood did. But Jesus saw her, called her, spoke to her, and laid his hands on her and immediately she was made straight (Luke 13:12-13 NIV). Not the next day, or the next seven days, or next year. The Bible says immediately she was made straight. WOW!

Jesus had and gave the one touch she desperately needed to make her whole again. His touch, in that moment, restored her joy, value, self-esteem, mind and soul back to life. His touch removed the grips of Hell that caused her to live in agony, weariness, and tiredness, for the last eighteen years. Jesus' physical contact – touch – had the sufficient power to reach where no other could have. One touch, in one day brought about the healing, miracle, answer, attention, approval, that she had been seeking in eighteen years. Will today be the day you say, "Enough is enough?" Will you be ready for your moment? Don't let your moment pass by because of your present situation. Stand even though you want to die. Shout in rejoice, even though you want to sit and cry. Arise. Be on the lookout for your moment is only around the corner. In the book of Jeremiah, the prophet gives some comforting words to the people of Israel in the midst of a difficult time. He says in Jeremiah 29:11:

> "For I know the thoughts that I think toward
> you, saith the Lord, thoughts of peace, and not
> of evil, to give you an expected end."

I know it's hard to believe and comprehend that Gods thoughts and plans for your life may include some of the unimaginable and unspeakable things you've had to face in life. But to know that He has an expected end for you, is more than enough to know that you will not die in the midst of pain, tragedy, adversity, trial. Little did Leah know that God was paying close attention to every detail of her life and that soon He would do something on her behalf. How great it is to serve a God who knows when and how to work on our behalf? He tells us to stand still and see the salvation of the Lord (Psalm 46:10). There is no need to worry about anything, no matter how difficult it may be or feel because in due season if we faint not, we shall see our reward (Galatians 6:9). Leah, despite feeling left out,

abandoned, unloved, mistreated, she never stopped performing her duties.

Let's be honest, this wasn't and isn't an easy thing to do.
It's not easy to serve or perform when one isn't validated. But
she continued, day in and day out, as she was so desperate
in gaining Jacob's love. This is what perseverance looks like.
Ultimately it will pay off, not as you want or expect but as
God sees fit. And it is in the midst of her pain that God
begins to refresh her weary soul by allowing her womb to
bare children. The word for weary is 'aphah, which comes
from the root word 'ayeph. This could also mean thirsty. It
is a word used by desert dwellers. As we rarely experience
a life-threatening thirst, we just have one word for thirsty.
People living in the desert are always thirsty, so they have
two words. The normal everyday thirst in Hebrew is tsama'
but when you are really thirsty, ready to faint from thirst
that is 'aphah. In fact, 'aphah is a play on the word da'avah
used at the end of the verse meaning to faint (Jeremiah
31:25). How do you satisfy someone who is fainting? Give
them what they need, either plenty of air or water.[15] Where
do you go when you are tired, thirsty or in a need? What
do you do when you feel as if you can't take another step
forward? Who do you call for help?

The Bible tells us in Psalms 42:1 that the psalmist in
the midst of his need, cries out to God in the same manner
that a deer does for water. The water has a twofold function.

A deer not only seeks for water to quench its thirst, but to refresh its body from the bad scent it releases that attracts predators. Some of its main predators consists of—humans, gray wolves, mountain lions, coyotes, bears and jaguars—all of which are considered to be wild animals. The Bible says in 1 Peter 5:8-9, "Be sober, be vigilant; because your adversary the devil, as a roaring lion, walketh about, seeking whom he may devour: Whom resist steadfast in the faith, knowing that the same afflictions are accomplished in your brethren that are in the world." It is why the psalmist expresses to God, the fountain of living water that only He has what his weary soul needs in order to recover and the ability to standfast.

We also find another interesting account in The Bible that describes an encounter Jesus had with a Samaritan woman in John 4. The chapter begins by providing details about Jesus' return back to Galilee from Judaea, and His "need" to go through Samaria. What's so important about this? This woman needed to know that the water she continues to draw from was not doing anything for her. In fact, she continues to lose herself with each drink. You must understand that Jesus wasn't referring to the water from the well of Jacob. Jesus was talking about the water she found in her multiple partners. His "need" to go through Samaria, was to rescue this woman from the scent of "shame" that kept lurking the predator of her soul and keeping her as his prey. Jesus wanted this woman to know that He was the only one who could provide and do for her what nobody else could. He wanted her eyes to be opened to know that there is a way out from the lifestyle she had been living in and no longer working for her. This woman was very known in her days, but not how you really want to be known. She had been with five different men, and the one who she was living with at the time wasn't her husband. It's very easy to cover up our hurts, wounds, needs, so that no one knows, but there is nothing that escapes the eye of our Lord. He knows how to make it on time. He is never late or too early. He's an on-time God, who knows exactly what is needed. However, the choice is always left to us to make. What will yours be today? I believe you have what it takes to turn your situation around.

Let's go back to Leah and see how she did it. After many unsuccessful attempts at trying to live life while lost, Leah realizes that lifestyle wasn't working out. Something needed to change. The process of change isn't pleasurable. Change begins to take place as a result of the process. Both –process and change—are two painful events that if endured, will provide life rewarding effects. Let's take a deeper look at these two separately:

- **Process:** is defined as a series of actions or steps taken in order to achieve a particular end. It's etymology states that it is an early fourteenth century word, *rocess*, "Fact of being carried on" (as in *in process*), from Old French *rocess* "A journey; continuation, development; legal trial" (13c.) and directly from Latin *processus* "A going forward, advance, progress, "From past-participle stem of *precedere* "go forward" (see proceed)[16].

In Jeremiah 29:11, God spoke a word to His people while they were captive in Babylon. The word was to instill hope and to remind his people that no matter what the present situation looked like. His plan was to give them an expected end. We often tend to complain and curse the situations we live through because of how they make us feel in the moment, not realizing that that "particular" situation is being allowed and used by God for the expected end he has for us.

Actually, one meaning of the word "good" in Hebrew is, "Capable of accomplishing God's designed purpose."[17] That's right. He is going to use that which was meant to break you, harm you and kill you for His good. Go ahead and ask Joseph in Genesis 37, how did God used his brother's betrayal for good? But many years later he tells them all in Genesis 50:20,

"You intended to harm me, but God intended
it for good to accomplish what is now being
done, the saving of many lives."

Prior to the process,
God gave Joseph a
dream. The dream was
to serve him as hope of Gods *"expected end."* Hope is
not wishful thinking. Hope is the assurance that whatever comes your way, or what you may face, you're
making it to the "end." Nothing can or will be able to
stop you in the process.

> Hope is not
> wishful thinking.

The "processes" in Joseph's life was to prepare and
equip him to serve both effectively and efficiently in
the calling over his life. Therefore, the processes we face
in life aren't designed to kill us, rather to help us reach
our fullest potential that we may become vessels readily
available to serve and accomplish that which we have
been created for. In order to reach that particular end,
one must be willing to adapt no matter how uncomfortable the process might make us feel. If we fail to adapt,
we will find ourselves repeating certain things in life
until that end has been reached.

I remember one day. In fact, it was a Memorial Day weekend, when the Lord gave me a lesson about his purpose regarding the "process" in my life. In my conversation with Him that day, I questioned so many events I had been through along with the ones I was experiencing and didn't want to even think about the ones I would face tomorrow. I was so frustrated. And in the middle of this conversation, the Lord interrupted to let me know what the issue was. He told me the reason of my frustration was due to me holding on to things He wanted to strip from me during the processes I had been facing in order to step into the next level he had prepared for me. That's right, I was the problem. Not the devil, not God, not my husband or children, it was ME. I felt the process was killing me while in reality it was serving its purpose, but I wasn't willing to change.

One of the purposes for the process is to show what is harbored in your heart (Deut. 8:2). Yeah, I know you think your heart is clean and pure, but you'll be surprised with the things we hold on to that God wants to change. The process stage will prepare you to make the changes needed for what comes next. You cannot move forward freely when you are carrying a load of baggage. Next stage requires you pack light.

• **Change:** is defined as a transformation or modification; alteration. The root word for change is "to become different, be altered." Someone once said, there is no change without loss. In other words, change requires that you let go of the old in order to receive the new. To let go of the thing not working and give a try to that which will give the expected end.

Change is the reflection of that which has taken place within. You will never be able to change that which you won't confront. And in order to confront it, you must identify it and to identify you must be willing to allow the process to play its course. In the book of Joshua 1:8, God told him to meditate *"purposefully"* on the word day and night. Why? Meditation is known as a practice that uses various techniques to train the attention and awareness, and to achieve a mentally clear and emotional calm and stable state.

Meditation, therefore, brings about a change in the way you perceive yourself, others and life. Joshua had a task at hand as the successor of Moses and in order to fulfill the job his well-being needed to be aligned both physically, mentally, and spiritually to the word. There was not room for doubts if he was the man of the hour. There was no room for uncertainties about his future and the people of Israel. He needed to meditate on the word and allow the word to permeate his mind and soul to bring about the visible change that was produced in his inner man. Change requires we break out of a wrong mind set or thinking process of who we are and what we've been called to do.

Like Joshua, oftentimes we feel inadequate for the task because we tend to compare with the leader who was prior to us. Joshua knew how well Moses served God and the people. He must had been carrying a secret conflict that only was naked before the eye of the Lord. It is why I believe the Lord told him three times to be "strong and courageous" (Joshua 1:6,7,9). I dare you this day, to try it again. Change the attitude of your heart from negative to positive, change your thoughts about things you don't understand, change the way you speak about yourself, your family, or your issues. Dare to tell them all, ***God has an expected end for me***, and I shall not die, but live, and declare the works of the Lord (Psalm 118:17).

Have you had quite enough of the same results? Investing so much time, effort, and energy and still in the same situation? Are you ready for a change? We often think and talk about the change we want and desire, but we never fully act upon it.

Listen, I used to have an attitude problem. Yes, you read that right. I said used to. Through the constant meditation on the word of God and the determination to change, today I can say (and those who know me well) that I am not who I used to be. My attitude was so stinking bad that my family and close friends would dread to be around me. It wasn't because they didn't love, it was because they did not know what would trigger me to explode. Whenever I would explode, it was downhill from there. If I felt you looked at me the wrong way, or you said something that rubbed me the wrong way, it was World War III. This might sound funny, but it isn't a joke. To me everybody else had a problem but not me. Everybody needed to change but not me. And don't you dare get caught trying to tell me that I had an attitude problem, because you wouldn't live to see the sunshine the next day.

All of this that would cause an explosion on the outside was a result of the inner turmoil I was facing. I was broken, hurt, angry, lost, and honestly just tired. Part of the frustration I mention earlier had to do with everything that was taking place inside of me. As I faced the different processes, I would become more frustrated because instead of seeing change, I would fall into the same rut. But I remember one day, I got tired of it all. I remember waking up that day and standing in front of the mirror not liking the reflection I saw. I couldn't stand the person I had allowed myself to turn into. I was bitter and miserable, and I could not bear that weight any longer. Shortly thereafter, I found myself on the living room floor, bowed down before God in humiliation. It is here that I learned I had the power to turn my story around. My turning point started the minute I identify that the problem lied in me.

Change did not happen overnight. **Change was progressive.** Nonetheless, it happened. It wasn't easy, but I did it. I learned that all things work together for good according to Romans 8:28 and Colossians 1:16-17. He knows how it all will work out for his final purpose. Though we may not understand half the time the why's of the process, declare as Job did in Job 23:10 (NIV):

> "But he knows the way that I take; when he has tested me, I will come forth as gold."

To be found is a decision to submit and surrender all control to the sovereignty of God. To be found, is to position yourself in the place that you can be found in Him. There is no place, like

> There is no place, like to the one you come to where you surrender into the hands of the potter.

to the one you come to where you surrender into the hands of the potter.

Bounce Back

CHAPTER 4

I Can, I Will

*And Leah conceived, ... And she conceived again,...
And she conceived again,...And she conceived
again, ...Genesis 29: 32 – 35*

W HEN DOES ENOUGH become enough? What does "enough" actually mean? Everyone has a different threshold for when enough becomes enough. For instance, what may look like enough to you in a particular situation may not be the same for someone else. Yet, it comes a time where we all, independently of whatever the situation may be, will experience some degree of tiredness, fatigue, and exhaustion, causing that a change take place in our lives.

I could remember like yesterday, standing in the middle of my kitchen in disbelief that once again, I was in the same situation I had been in the last three years. As panic, worry, and uncertainty began to find a way into my heart, with tears flowing down my face, I looked at my husband and said, I refuse to live another year like this. Let me explain. For the last three years, right around September through December, we would find ourselves living from one source of income which wasn't enough to get by. We were forced to ask for help from family members, our church and even had to apply for government assistance. There were count-less nights, where I would cry myself to sleep after seeing the results from the monthly budget. I'd play the "eeny, meeny, miny, moe" song as I looked through the pile of bills to see which one would get paid and which one would be placed on hold.

Now, I was facing year number four this time. I knew something had to change but didn't quite know what or how. The next couple of days, I found myself trapped between all sorts of thoughts. Where is God? Why is this happening again? I'm a failure and we're never getting out of this. My stomach would cringe at the mere thought of people's reaction when finding out that once again we were in the same situation. I even found myself trying to figure out what had happened with the relief I apparently felt once the need had been met and resolved from previous years. As I fought between these thoughts and feeling, I remembered a story I'd read in a Christian magazine about a family who had gone through what my family and I were experiencing. I could remember having this inner conversation with myself about whether God would be able to come through for us as he had done with this family.

One evening, after work, I made a quick stop at the nearest dollar store and bought all the sticky pads I could find. I spent the next several days searching all of God's promises found in The Bible and wrote them on a sticky note. I gathered my family – my two little boys at the time and husband – to inform them the plan and strategy we were taking this year to break the cycle we had been under. I didn't want a quick solution that would only anesthetize the situation, I wanted a long-life solution. My husband thought I had gone crazy, but I knew and believed that God wasn't a receptor of man that He is willing and able to do greater than what I ask or imagine. This was my time, to come to know and experience God as I'd never had before. I'm so sure that if I had not taken this approach, I would had lived yet another year in the same situation.

But as Leah's' declaration in Genesis 29:35, I said this time I will do it differently.

This was the order:

1. **Do not share or comment with anyone outside this home about the situation we are facing.**

I was determined in seeing God's work in our lives. Spending time in scriptures had opened my eyes to learn that God isn't too far away from his children in times of need. Scriptures like these helped me keep my focus and trust on God:

> But without faith it is impossible to please him:
> for he that cometh to God must believe that he
> is, and that he is a rewarder of them that dili-
> gently seek him. – Hebrew 11:6

> For the word of God is quick, and powerful,
> and sharper than any two-edged sword,
> piercing even to the dividing asunder of soul
> and spirit, and of the joints and marrow, and
> is a discerner of the thoughts and intents of the
> heart. – Hebrews 4:12

So shall my word be that goeth forth out of my mouth: it shall not return unto me void, but it shall accomplish that which I please, and it shall prosper in the thing whereto I sent it. – Isaiah 55:11

but thou, when thou prayest, enter into thy closet, and when thou hast shut thy door, pray to thy Father which is in secret; and thy Father which seeth in secret shar reward thee openly. – Mathew 6:6

But seek ye first the kingdom of God, and his righteousness; and all these things shall be added unto you. – Mathew 6:33

2. **Grab as much sticky note you can in your hands.**

This was like the order the widow in 2 King 4 received from Elisha. This was a matter of life or death.

And Elisha said unto her, "What shall I do for thee? Tell me, what hast thou in the house?" And she said, "Thine handmaid hath not anything in the house, save a pot of oil." Then he said, "Go, borrow thee vessels abroad of all thy neighbors, even empty vessels; borrow not a few. And when thou art come in, thou shalt shut the door upon thee and upon thy sons, and shalt pour out into all those vessels, and thou shalt set aside that which is full." So, she went from him, and shut the door upon her and upon her sons, who brought the vessels to her; and she poured out. – 2 Kings 4:2–5

3. **Place them all over the house (walls, doors, cabinets, windows, appliances).**

The placing of the sticky note was critically important. It needed to be in a place that was visible to everyone. What good is it to have something and not be able to use it because you forgot where you placed it? The following passage in scriptures taught me the importance of God's word and led me to this act of faith.

Hear, O Israel: The LORD our God is one LORD: And thou shalt love the LORD thy God with all thine heart, and with all thy soul, and with all thy might. And these words, which I command thee this day, shall be in thine heart: And thou shalt teach them diligently unto thy children, and shalt talk of them when thou sittest in thine house, and when thou walkest by the way, and when thou liest down, and when thou risest up. And thou shalt bind them for a sign upon thine hand, and they shall be as frontlets between thine eyes. And thou shalt write them upon the posts of thy house, and on thy gates. – Deuteronomy 6:4–9

4. **Every time you pass by a sticky note, you are to read it out loud and send a praise of thanksgiving up to heaven.**

This wasn't an easy task. See, it's always easy to praise God when He has come through, but when you still are waiting its quite challenging to say, thank you for what you are about to do. Here are a few more scriptures that helped me while I waited on the Lord.

My God shall supply all your need according to his riches in glory by Christ Jesus. – Philippians 4:19

In everything give thanks: for this is the will of God in Christ Jesus concerning you. – 1 Thessalonians 5:18

> Be careful for nothing; but in everything by prayer and supplication with thanksgiving let your requests be made known unto God. – Philippians 4:6

I told my family two things I expect to see as of result of this act:

1. The enemy fleeing away.

It is Jesus who teaches us what it is to stand with our loins girded in the truth of God's word, while He was tempted in the wilderness.

> Then was Jesus led up of the Spirit into the wilderness to be tempted of the devil. And when He had fasted forty days and forty nights, he was afterward an hungered. And when the tempter came to him, he said, if thou be the Son of God, command that these stones be made bread. But He answered and said, it is written, man shall not live by bread alone, but by every word that proceedeth out of the mouth of God. Then the devil taketh Him up into the holy city, and setteth Him on a pinnacle of the temple, and saith unto Him, if thou be the Son of God,

cast thyself down: for it is written, He shall give His angels charge concerning thee: and in their hands they shall bear thee up, lest at any time thou dash thy foot against a stone. Jesus said unto him, it is written again, thou shalt not tempt the Lord thy God. Again, the devil taketh Him up into an exceeding high mountain, and sheweth him all the kingdoms of the world, and the glory of them; and saith unto him, all these things will I give thee, if thou wilt fall down and worship me. Then saith Jesus unto him, get thee hence, Satan: for it is written, thou shalt worship the Lord thy God, and him only shalt thou serve. Then the devil leaveth Him, and, behold, angels came and ministered unto Him. – Matthew 4:1 – 11

Submit yourselves therefore to God. Resist the devil, and he will flee from you. – James 4:7

2. Experiencing God in a supernatural way.

I told my husband, if God is who He says He is – *provider, owner of silver and gold, help in time of need, peace, way maker* – then He is the only one that can turn this situation around. It's one thing to know God based on what you read in the bible or hear every Sunday in a sermon, however, it's so much different to know Him through an experience.

> *I have heard of thee by the hearing of the ear: but now mine eye seeth thee.—Job 42:5*

> *Seek ye the Lord while he may be found, call ye upon him while he is near:—Isaiah 55:6*

> *Ask, and it shall be given you; see, and ye shall find; knock, and it shall be opened unto you: for every one that asketh receiveth; and he that seeketh findeth; and to him that knocketh it shall be opened. – Matthew 7:7-8*

Rest assured that God showed up and showed off. While we were down to the last gallon of water, yet with hearts full of expectancy, **God made a way**. A pastor who we'd known for years arrived at our home out of nowhere with a box full of food. If, that wasn't enough, the next day we received in the mail a check from an unknown person. And to top it all off, every time we would apply for government assistance, we were denied due to our income exceeded the limits. This time, they had approved our application for food stamps, and we had received a large amounts of foods stamps to last us the next couple of months. Talk about God's faithfulness.

Have you ever had a dream, vision, idea, or goal of achieving something extraordinary but found that as you stretched forth to grab it, you couldn't? As if, something literally pulls you right back and traps you in the same place. It's like going around and around the same mountain, day after day, week after week, month after month and year after year.

Cycles are a series of events that are regularly repeated in the same order. The main issue with cycles is that it can detour you off course and cause you to eventually forfeit your destiny. As crazy as that sounds, you can find yourself selling short of what God has destined for you since the foundation of the earth. The hardest step in breaking a cycle is the identification process. Why is this hard? This process, which by the way, is the first step, requires you to take a deep and close look at yourself. It's easy to look and point out other people's issues, but when we must look at our own it's difficult. I could only imagine what that group of Jews were thinking when Jesus told them in John 8:32,

> And ye shall know the truth, and the truth shall make you free.

We all may like the idea to confront an opposing party, especially when they have done us wrong. But what happens when that opposing party is yourself? What will you do today? Are you ready to confront yourself and break the cycles? Through her first three pregnancies, we see right into her heart. She longed for her husband Jacob to see her, hear her, and ultimately unite with her. While she sought day in and day out to be seen, heard and united, she failed to realize that God had seen her, heard her and was more united to her than she could imagine.

Oftentimes, we find ourselves like Leah, trying over and over to gain something from someone who cannot do for us that which only God can. Somewhere in between the *–lost and found stage*—Leah became tired of the old and of the repeated cycles and was ready to embrace that "expected end" the Lord had for her. We know that something happened during the fourth pregnancy, due to her declaration in verse 35. She had reached her threshold point of "enough." She realized that no one, not even Hell itself could stop her from reaching that which she was created for. She understood that she can change, and she did change (I can; I will). By positioning herself on the center of the potter's wheel, surrendering her will, her wants, her desires, and her thoughts, she was able to get a glimpse of the vision the potter had. She learned that she had more to offer than what she had lost.

In the book of Isaiah 42:9, God said:

"See, the former things have taken place, and
new things I declare; before they spring into
being, I announce them to you".

While you and I are going through the cycles of life,
God is working on our behalf. He is cleaning and pre-
paring everything in our life and path for that "transitional
moment" just as he did with Leah. God never slumbers or
sleeps according to Psalm 121:4. He is working and at work
despite us not being able to see Him. While we sleep, He
is up, stitching things together for us. While we are crying
over the hurts, pain, betrayals, and so forth, God is working.
No matter what the present situation may look like or be
like, we must know that God is working and soon we will
see it spring into being.

Have you ever studied the life cycle of a butterfly? It's
quite fascinating if you asked me. Not many are familiar
with process the butterfly endures to become this beautiful, colorful, and vibrant creature. The butterfly under-
goes four different stages in its life cycle ending with a
complete transformation during its last stage called metamorphosis. Metamorphosis is a word derived from Greek

origin meaning to change form or shape or a transformation. There are two types of Metamorphosis: *Complete and Incomplete.*

- ***Complete Metamorphosis***: Organisms that undergo complete metamorphosis are called "holometabolous," from the Greek words "holo" for "complete" or "whole," "meta" for "change," and the noun "bole" for "to throw." "Homometabolous," then means "completely changing," or "wholly changing."

- ***Incomplete Metamorphosis***: In this process, only some parts of the animal's body change during metamorphosis. Animals that only partially change their bodies as they mature are called "Hemimetabolous," from the Greek words "hemi" for "half," "meta," for "change," and the verb "bole" for "to throw." "Hemimetabolous," then, is a word meaning "half-changing."[18]

Although the metamorphosis process is not one that humans experience in their lifetime as seen in insects and most amphibians, there is much we can learn and relate to its radical transformation. Butterflies since day one of its existence are faced with the process of change. In order to become what they have been destined to be; they must undergo a series of changes. These changes do not happen overnight. However, each stage has its unique timing. None of these stages can be skipped. And it is during the last stage where the "metamorphosis" takes place, as the caterpillar finds a twig or safe place on the tree, where it spends the next couple of days or months transforming into that which we know–Butterfly.

Once this transformation is complete, the butterfly could never go back to what it used to be. In fact,

> Metamorphosis is a remarkable process.

during the first three stages, they are found to be restricted to the same place, a leaf. But once they transform into a butterfly, nothing holds them back. They are free to fly and go where they couldn't before. Metamorphosis is a remarkable process. You and I experience a similar transformation. Our transformation is done by the renewing of our mind according to Paul in Romans 12:2. I believe Leah positioned herself as the caterpillar did when it was ready to change. As the caterpillar finds that secure place, Leah found security in the secret place of the Most High, and in return He provided His shadow to serve as her protection, Psalms 91. Protection? From what? Protection against anything and everything that would hinder the moment of transformation, the transitional point from one stage to the other, just as the hardened case forms around the pupa to protect it from predators and extreme weathers.[19]

I want to ask you to do something right now. Are you ready? It may sound crazy to you, but please give a try. Are you ready? Ok, here it goes. Stop what you are doing. Head to the nearest place with a mirror. Look dead straight at yourself and repeat the following: "I can, and I will." Say it again, "I can, and I will." Now, say it again but this time fill in the blanks. What can you do and what will you do? "I can (blank) and I will (blank)." I believe that you can do it. If you can see yourself there, then you certainly can do it. Think about it for a moment.

Imagine for just a second what will happen to the caterpillar if it refuses to change and decides to stay as is –a *caterpillar*? It will die as a caterpillar, with so much beauty trapped inside. You were blessed with all blessings in the heavenly places

> Your now is only the prelude to where God is taking you.

according to Ephesians 1:3. Therefore, don't be afraid of change or get comfortable with where you at now. Your now is only the prelude to where God is taking you. You now may not even add up to what you see yourself doing in the future. Even if you can't see it right, God does, and He will surprise you. It is why I urge you my dear friend, do not quit now. Find your place in the Lord and position yourself as Leah did and give it another try. Don't give up in the *in between* process of change. Do you know when Leah's transformation was seen? It was seen right after she "tried again." That's right, it was seen after she conceived her fourth child after. Yes, she was the same woman, wife, sister, daughter, and friend but with a different attitude about herself and the world.

When you experience a "metamorphosis," it's impossible to go back to what was before. It's not that you can't go back, but when you do you'll find that you are unable to function at that level. You've been exposed to greater and the old will no longer satisfy. In 2 Corinthians 5:17(NIV), the apostle Paul wrote,

> Therefore, if anyone is in Christ, the new creation has come: The old has gone, the new is here!

The evidence of her transformation is not only seen by what she declared in Genesis 29:35, "This time I will praise," but by what the writer states at the end of that verse "then she stopped having children." What does this mean? She no longer went back to the old. She found in God through praise what she had lost many years ago. The power of praise is far greater than what we can imagine. Praise helped her connect with God and to bounce back to whom she truly was. She stopped having children under the old cycle. Don't be afraid and undergo the metamorphosis stage and I guarantee you that your life will never be the same. Let's take a closer look at her children before and after Judah.

Children born before Judah (Genesis 29: 31-35):

- Ruben "See Me"
- Simeon "Hear Me"
- Levi "Attach or Unite with Me"
- Judah "Praise"

Children born after Judah (Genesis 30:9-21):

- Gad "Good fortune or a troop"
- Asher "Happy"
- Issachar "Reward"
- Zebulun "Honor"

There are over 17,000 species of butterflies in the world and yet not two are same. They all go through the same cycle and process but at the end they all hold and display its own glory and beauty. The same goes with you and I, we may look the same, speak the same language, like the same things yet we each have our own unique set of characteristics that the world around us needs to see. Bounce back and know that if Leah could break her cycle so can you. Bounce back and know that if I could break my cycle so can you. You can and you will become that which you were created and destined for.

To sum it all up, in order to break a cycle or become the change you want to see, the below can serve as a guide to get you there.

1. Identify it.
2. Confront it.
3. Overcome it.

The breaking of a cycle is life changing not only to you but to those connected to you. Therefore, what you don't identify and confront to overcome, those con-

> The breaking of a cycle is life changing not only to you but to those connected to you.

nected to you will have to after you are gone. Don't give your cycles, patterns, or habits power and authority over you and your situation. In the book of Judges, we find the second generation of the people who was delivered from Egypt, living in the promised land, repeating the same vicious cycle according to Judges 2:10-23. Our children are a reflection of who we are. If you and I chose not to break the cycles in our lives, imagine how their future will be. Go ahead, think about that. Did you like what you saw? What you do and how you do it, plays a huge impact on those coming after you.

In the days of the Judges, this was a new generation who did not know neither the Lord nor what he had done for Israel. How is that even possible? Can you remember everything the Lord had done for his people? He delivered them from Egypt with a strong hand, sending ten different plagues. He parted the Red Sea in half so that a multitude of people can cross to the other side on dry land. He swallowed up the Egyptians and their chariots that were coming right after them while crossing the sea. He provided food and water in the desert for forty years. Their clothes didn't go bad all that time either. He became a pillar of fire at night to keep them warm and pillar of cloud to protect against the scorching sun during the day. This is what we read in The Bible, but who knows all the other things God did for them that wasn't registered and yet, there is a new generation who doesn't know about the Lord nor what he has done. When was the last time you shared with your family something God did for you?

CHAPTER 5

There Is No Place Like Home

Life takes you to unexpected places, love brings you home.[20] –Unknown Author

BOUNCING BACK FOR most may seem like an unimaginable reality. Who can bounce back from loss? How can one bounce back? Bounce back to what? Questions like this and more are asked and pondered by those who have experienced some type of loss in their life. At least we know of one person, Naomi. Let's take a dive into one of the bittersweet books found in The Bible where the Lord in spite of the present condition and situation, displays a picture of what redemption would look like for us all.

The book of Ruth takes place during one of the darkest periods of the nation of Israel. During this period, the book of Judge tells us twice that due to the lack of a king, each man did as they saw right in their eyes (Judges 17:16; 21:25). This is very dangerous. You'll also find in the book of Proverbs two verses where King Solomon expresses about that which may seem right unto man (Proverbs 14:12; 16:25). I've come to learn that that which is mentioned more than once, requires my full attention, and must not be ignored. And if I were to go any deeper, I would say that when studying the word of God, we must not ignore that which requires our fullest attention. When God delivered his people from Egypt, they sojourned in the wilderness for about forty years. Those years were to prepare them for the possession of the promise land God had promised Abraham (Genesis 15:1-21).

Throughout their days in the wilderness, the Lord gave Moses precepts, ordinances, commandments and statues for his people, specific orders they needed to become acquainted with before entering into the promise land. One of the last task Moses fulfills before passing away is found in Deuteronomy 28. This passage clearly states the consequences that would follow in response to their decisions.

Their decision will not only impact their own lives but those connected to them. This is vitally important to know and understand. We often live our lives as though we are not accountable to anyone, and as if our decisions don't impact those around us. But there is one truth that we cannot escape from even if we tried, is that at the end of it all we must render counts to God for all our actions.

Therefore, one must not be too hasty when it comes to making a decision. Decisions should be well thought out. On this note, I bring you back to the book of Ruth, where we learn about the effect and impact a decision has in our lives and those

> One must not be too hasty when it comes to making a decision.

connected to us. As a result of the first decision, the small-town family of Bethlehem is strike with tragedy. Elimelech, whose name means *"My God is King,"* is from the tribe of Ephraim and has made from what it seems a *"reasonable decision"* in his eyes, by moving his family from Bethlehem to the country of Moab. The move according to The Bible had to do with a famine the land was experiencing at the time. You may think and ask, how bad can a move be? What can go wrong from moving from place A to place B? Sadly, for this family it went terribly wrong. What they saw and interpreted as "good" ended up being what we would say "the worst decision ever." After all, it's only supposed to be temporary. He is only seeking substance for his family, due to the famine that was taking place in Bethlehem.

> Trust in the Lord with all thine heart; and lean not unto thine own understanding. In all thy ways acknowledge him, and he shall direct thy paths. Be not wise in thine own eyes: fear the Lord, and depart from evil. It shall be health to thy navel, and marrow to thy bones. (Proverbs 3:5-8 KJV)

My friend, we are encouraged in Proverbs 3:5-8 to lean on the Lord and not our own understanding. Do you know how many headaches we can avoid if only we learn to wait? I know, it's not easy to wait. We don't like it and if we can avoid it, we will. But waiting has its rewards. There is nothing like waiting on the Lord and his timing. His timing is perfect. He is an on-time God. You can count on Him being on time. He is never too late nor too early. If there is anyone that can testify on God's timing is King David (Psalm 40:1-4). And when he shows up, there is nothing or no one that can stop Him from working on your behalf. There is no situation too big for Him to handle. There is no sickness that He can't heal. There are no chains He can't break. There is nothing that He can't resolve. Your God has always existed. No one created Him. He controls everything above, on and beneath the earth. The earth is His and everything and everyone in it (Psalm 24:1).

When we read the accounts of the creation in Genesis, we find that when God began to create, the first thing he said was "Let there be light" (Genesis 1:3). That light caused the darkness to dissipate. Why? God wanted you to know, as you read his word, that no matter what situation has darkened your life, He and only He has the power to dispel that which wants to overpower you. Listen to me, your God, is an awesome God. He will not waste your time. Therefore, wait on Him. Wait on His response, wait on His approval, wait on His timing. Don't do as Elimelech, who thought his decision was better than what God had planned for him and his family. Let me explain something here. The problem with his move had to do with his intention. He was attempting to escape the one who had allowed the famine—God. God was dealing with his people through the famine. His people had turned away from Him again and was living according to their own desires. They had forgotten what Moses had spoken in Deuteronomy 28. You and I may forget God's word and commandments from time to time, but God never forgets. He holds true to everything he says. Yet I'm blown by how God works and does his works. It's incomprehensible and at the same time undoubtable that there is a God who is Sovereign. God is a fair God.

I say this to point out that although God was dealing with His people as an all. He knew who are the ones that are living right versus the ones who weren't. Needless to say, when God was dealing with Pharaoh to let his people go, He sent ten different plagues on separate occasions. Mind you, God's people were living in the same land as the Egyptians during this time, but while the plagues were devastating everything in the land, the Lord simultaneously provided covering for his people in Goshen (Exodus 8:22-23). God provided protection to his people who were in the same

> God provided protection to his people who were in the same land at the same time as the plague was.

land at the same time as the plague was. Today, God is able to do the same for us. Whatever the situation may be that you are facing today, don't make a decision that will cause you to lose more than what you have. In the midst of the things we don't understand, let's take Habakkuk's position. He asked of the Lord, waited on the Lord, and did as the Lord instructed (Habakkuk 2:1-4). It's time we learn to wait on the Lord and trust that He will provide and make a way for us as we wait.

As Elimelech and his family sojourn to Moab, little did they know that Naomi, whose name means *pleasant* or *sweet*, would become a bitter childless widow. That the so-called land that had what they needed "now" would be the same place where she would lose it all. In fact, what supposed to be a temporary move, turned out to be a stay of ten years. Ten years away from home and of those she knew. Ten years where she experienced loss after loss and has become bitter in the process. Naomi finds herself facing the effects of the decision her husband made, alone, in a strange land, with two Moabite girls who her sons had married. We don't know how long they were married. However, we do know that they too are suffering the loss of their husbands. I can only imagine all the questions that bombarded Naomi's mind through this time. Why is this happening to me? Why now? Why me? Where is God? Where do I go now? What will I do? How can I possibly bounce back from this?

If you can relate to these questions, know that there is a way out and that you, just like Naomi, can bounce back. You may think, how? Naomi shows us how. As a matter of fact, the same way into Moab was the same way out. She makes a decision to return back home (Ruth 1:6). Through her decision, she lets us know that there is no place like home. Home for me is the place I feel safe, secure, and comfortable. It's where I can be me. Home is more than just a house. A house is that which occupies a space in a certain place or location. While on the other hand, a home is not necessarily subject to a specific place or location.

The promised land was given to the Israelites as a place to become their home. However, they lost their home as a result of their wrong choices and decisions. Yet, we find in Jeremiah 29 a promise that the Lord will bring them back to their home after a determined timeframe (Jeremiah 29:10). While they spent the next seventy years in a foreign and pagan land, the Lord instructed them to build houses to dwell in them. In other words, this will become your new home. You know what made the house in Babylon their "home?" God's involvement. God was the center of it all. His presence is home! It was in knowing that God had visited His people that prompt Naomi to take a stand and return back home. She was heading back to the place where everything was working out well until that famine period. She was going back to Bethlehem, which means *House of God* located in Judah, which means *praise*. She was going back to the house of God where his praise changes everything. Praise break!

His presence is home!

Nothing like to be in the house of the Lord surrounded by praises. The psalmist said in Psalms 122:1,

> I was glad when they said unto me, let us go
> into the house of the Lord.

Why? Something happens in the house of the Lord when his people gather with a sound of praise. There is healing, deliverance, transformation, restoration, and freedom. It's almost impossible for you not to be changed. She could had settled and remained in Moab. After all, there really wasn't anything or anyone waiting for her at home. She had no one to tend to her. To provide for her. She had no security for her future. Yet, despite all the "cons" she was facing, she pushes through and prepares to leave Moab. Despite losing her loved ones in Moab, she didn't want to die in that place. The only thing she leaves in Moab is her footsteps. Why? So that the next person who comes through can know that there is a way out. That you can bounce back from loss, from despair, from loneliness, from confusion, from depression and bitterness. You don't have to lose it all in Moab when God shows up at home. It's time to take out the red shoes from our closet's and like Dorothy from the movie "The Wizard of Oz" click them three times and say, "There is no place like home." You'll find others who just like Naomi, in the midst of their darkest hour, they decide to return home:

> There is no place like home.

- *The prodigal son (Luke 15:11-32)*: He is the one who asked to receive his inheritance before time. Not because he was in a need, but because he wanted to be on his own. He thought that home was restricting him, while, in reality, it was protecting him. His father, who loved him more than what he could imagine, granted the son's petition. He gave him his portion of the inheritance. All we know next, is that the son left his home, squandered his wealth in reckless living and now is in a need (Luke 15:13-14 ESV). He probably thought that the inheritance would last longer than his father's home. But one day, he comes to his senses and decides to return back home. He realizes that there is no place like home. I'd rather be home and working with the servants than in the condition in which he'd find himself. He had reached rock bottom, but he found a way out. As he began to head home, thinking of what he would tell his father, unbeknownst to him, his father was waiting for him with open arms. This is the beauty of HOME. He could had allowed his pride and failure to keep him far away from home, yet he didn't, in fact he does what most are unwilling to do, "he gave it another try." He turned his story around. He refused to let the swine field be the last place he would see. He decided to take the same road that led him out into the country, back home. Are you willing to travel that same road, instead this time back home?

- *Jacob Returns Home (Genesis 27:1-35:29)*: He is ordered by God to return to the place he had abruptly left in an escape from his brother who sought to kill him. Yup! You read that right. Someone at *home* wanted to kill Jacob. He left his comfort, his parents, and friends behind because instead of waiting on the Lord and His timing, he took by deceit that which belonged to his brother. Yet, in order for God to fulfill His promise with Jacob (Genesis 28:10-22), he needed to return back home to face the reason why he had left. While he lived in Haran, working for his uncle Laban, the Lord watched over him and blessed him abundantly. In chapter 30 of Genesis, we find that Jacob is ready to go home, after all he has been in Haran about twenty years, but Laban isn't ready to let him go. Why would he? He was being blessed as a result of the promise of the Lord over Jacob's life. Nevertheless, the Lord spoke to Jacob to let him know that it was time to return back home. I believe that Jacob's heart began to race with all kinds of emotions. But ultimately, the thought would never escape his mind, and he is faced with knowing that the day soon of confronting his past was soon approaching. It is why I believe the Lord told him as you return back home to the land of your father and grandfather "*I will be with you.*" Everything else after that shouldn't matter. Why? God has got it and He is control. Yes, I have to face the situation, but I won't be alone. That means that He will give me and equip me with everything I need for that moment. God dealt with Jacob as he lived Haran. He prepared him in the silent night hours, while he slept, for this encounter with his brother. And as he journeyed back home, thinking and seeing himself probably as the same person who had fled twenty years ago, the Lord allowed him to have a one on one encounter with the one who had bid him to return home. It was that night where Jacob died, and Israel was born. It was that night where Jacob past was dealt with and he was transformed into the man called and appointed by God. It's true he left that place limping, but he was a changed man.

As Naomi embarks her journey back home, she bids her two daughters-in-law twice to stay in Moab and to return back to their mother's house (Ruth 1:8). But the girls pleaded with Naomi to bid them not to stay. Naomi, who felt as she had nothing else to give them, insisted that they stay and return back to their formal life before the chaos. Really? Who can return to what they had before the divorce, the loss, the betrayal?

Well, Orpah did. She took Noemi's offer went back to what was familiar. She couldn't see past her pain nor her in-laws' pain. Therefore, she chose to return and to settle in familiarity. How many of us at times choose the easy way out? Yes, I know, Naomi did tell her twice to return, nonetheless, this was an opportunity to bear things out and give life a chance and a moment to discover something different. The uncertainty of moving forward to Naomi's "homeland" caused her to settle with what was normal. How many of us find ourselves forfeiting our moments because of the uncertainties of tomorrow? Orpah missed out on her moment. Don't decide to turn your back when given the opportunity for change because it doesn't look like what you think or was expecting. Don't miss it because you might not have another moment like that one.

On the other hand, Ruth, decided to stay with Noemi. Uncertain of what her tomorrow may bring or may look like, there is one thing she knows to be true, she does not want to stay in Moab. Ruth has decided to give life another try, this time, in Bethlehem located in Judah. There is nothing like defying the odds after a tragic event in life or failing repeatedly. She wanted to move forward, to have a change in scenery, a breath of fresh air and the opportunity to try again. We can wish for things to happen all day long and even speak about them, but if a step into that direction is not taken then nothing will happen nor change. The Bible does not provide much information of her upbringing nor who her parents and siblings were. However, it specifies that she was a Moabite. The Moabites were descendant of

Lot and one of Israel's main enemies. They were idolaters and very malicious people. Ruth, who had grown up in this atmosphere had had enough and saw in her marriage to Mahlon, who was the youngest son of Naomi, an opportunity for change. In Ruth's eyes, Mahlon became her deliverer or savior out of this nightmare she'd been living in.

Have you been in a situation where you had to abide by what others thought or believed? How many opportunities have you missed because it required you to move into an unfamiliar territory or to do something you are not used to or accustomed to? How many times have you said no to questions and open doors because you have felt inadequate or unworthy? Just as Ruth, Orpah had an opportunity of a lifetime to move forward and above all to experience the God of Israel but she chooses to settle in Moab. Why? Maybe because it was easier. Probably didn't believe she had what it took to try. Or was too afraid of the results. Unlike Ruth, who said to Naomi your God will now be my God and your people my people, Orpah responded by simply staying with her custom and belief.

Ruth seized her moment and wasn't going to let nobody, not even Naomi with her bitterness, take it away. There is nothing worse than to be around a bitter person. You don't know what to expect from a bitter person. One minute they can seem to be fine and the next minute they are gone with the wind. A bitter person will speak and act out from pain not realizing the implications or the impact that their words and or actions may have tomorrow. They can't see past the present moment they are living. Although Naomi didn't understand the bigger picture at hand, she had been sent on an assignment for such an hour as that to bring forth hidden treasures that were within these two young ladies. Sadly, we are unable to see that which was trapped in Orpah as she settled with so much beauty to give.

Therefore, know today that what you and I have within, is far greater than anything that wants us to negotiate to stay trapped and settle beneath our purpose in life. I don't know what Moab may represent in your life. But don't settle there. There is so much more for you in the world. It may require a little of sacrifice, but you will be far better off than settling. It's time to return to the house of the Lord with a praise of thanksgiving. No matter what you may have experience in life, He is still worthy of your praise. It could have killed you and it probably was designed to eliminate you, but you are still here. You are stronger, more knowledgeable and experienced. You are a living testimony that there is a light at the end of the tunnel. That weeping may endure for the night but Joy cometh in the morning (Psalm 30:5).

> It could have killed you and it probably was designed to eliminate you, but you are still here.

I can remember a time in my life where I couldn't see beyond what I was going through. I would question God day in and day out. After a whole lot of crying, praying, counseling, and praising I began to see that light. I literally thought that my life was over, that there was nothing left for me to do. I felt like Naomi, bitter, with the way life had treated me and at the same time, I felt like Ruth and Orpha where I needed to decide. Was I going to stay in Moab or was I going to move forward and trust the God of Israel? I, like Ruth, decided to trust God, the God my mother and grandmother faithfully served. I, like Naomi, decided to give life another try. I wiped the tears from my eyes, tried to hold all the broken pieces in place as I prepared to go back home. This time, I knew it had to be done differently. As I placed my trust in God, I allowed Him to lead the way as I humbly obeyed the tender and gentle voice of the Holy Spirit.

We are often encouraged and taught to prepare for success in every area of life and not for failure. We train and teach our children that if you follow A to Z everything will be okay. But what happens when things don't come out the way we planned? When life keeps taking us on a journey we didn't sign up for? We do not like these moments in life and tend to curse them. But it is through days and moment like those that allows us to know God at a deeper level. As I mentioned before, I went through a season in life that I thought I would never overcome. I was convinced that this was it. I now had to adjust at being a single mother of two and that no one would want a broken messed up church girl. Little did I know that this moment in life had been orchestrated by God himself and that he was using this life experience to teach me and my husband what marriage really was.

I remember like yesterday going to church with my two little ones. As we were exiting from Sunday school class, my husband happened to be entering the congregation. I found myself blushing and having butterflies, as if I was fifteen years old. I needed just a minute or two to adjust before entering the congregation. All the anger, pain, and resentment I felt toward him and the situation that led my marriage to fall apart had dissipated like vapor. I couldn't figure out why and that alone made me feel more nervous than anything. I build up the courage to greet my husband as I entered the church since it had been about seven months that I had not seen nor heard from Him. When we greeted, it was like love at first sight. This day was the beginning of something new the Lord was doing on our behalf. When I decided to give it another try to put behind me the pain of yesterday and to embrace the gift of today, was when I was able to walk into what the future held for me and my family.

As a result of my decision, my once broken and shambled marriage was now restored and better than what it was. Today my husband and I pastor a wonderful church, hold several marriage conferences, and have a stronger solid relationship that has been built upon the Lord Jesus Christ. This does not mean that we have it all together or that we don't face any struggles. Quite contrary, we have had a load of situations that at the time seemed unconquerable, but one thing we know that hasn't failed us, God is the solution. When it seems that we can't find the balance or harmony, we take a trip down to Bethlehem in Judah (House of the Lord – Praise) because there is no place like home.

The book of Ruth is an encouragement to us, especially when we feel uncertain of our future and unclear about the decisions to take. If Ruth was here with us today, I'm sure she would tell us that moving to Bethlehem was one of the best decisions she could have made in her life. Why? Though uncertain about what her future held in Naomi's homeland, as a Moabite and a widow, God rewarded her faith. God, who is the owner of the home, does what He wants whenever He wants and with whom He wants. I love this about our God. Everybody can have an opinion about you based on what they know, have seen or heard about your past or your family history, but at the end of the day what matters more is that which God has to say about you.

God doesn't consult anybody when He wants to bless you. He doesn't seek your spouse's, parents, relatives, friend's approval when he wants to bless, he simply opens the gate of heaven and pours down a blessing you aren't able to contain.

I believe it is why the apostle Paul wrote in 1 Corinthians 1:18 – 31 that God chose that which the world deemed unfit to glorify himself through.

> For the preaching of the cross is to them that perish foolishness; but unto us which are saved it is the power of God. For it is written, I will destroy the wisdom of the wise, and will bring to nothing the understanding of the prudent. Where is the wise? Where is the scribe? Where is the disputer of this world? Hath not God made foolish the wisdom of this world? For after that in the wisdom of God the world by wisdom knew not God, it pleased God by the foolishness of preaching to save them that believe. For the Jews require a sign, and the Greeks seek after wisdom: But we preach Christ crucified, unto the Jews and Greeks, Christ the power of God, and the wisdom of God. Because the foolishness of God is wiser than men; and the weakness of God is stronger than men. For ye see your calling, brethren, how that not many wise men after the flesh, not many mighty, not many noble, are called: But God hath chosen the foolish things of the world to confound the wise; and God hath chosen

the weak things of the world to confound the things which are mighty; And base things of the world, and things which are despised, hath God chosen, yea, and things which are not, to bring to nought things that are: That no flesh should glory in his presence. But of him are ye in Christ Jesus, who of God is made unto us wisdom, and righteousness, and sanctification, and redemption: That according as it is written, He that glorieth, let him glory in the Lord. 1 Corinthians 1:18-31

It was here in Bethlehem, the land God had visited to bless His people with bread, that Ruth met her Boaz. Boaz, whose name means *"strength is within him,"* is a picture of what Jesus would be for you and me. He provided security for their tomorrow. Boaz wasn't too concern with Ruth's past, her nationality or whether she had anything of value to provide. He had all that she needed. He had all that he needed.

Jesus, who is our Boaz, our redeemer, our kinsman, isn't too concern either with our past or our nationality-he is looking to provide us with security. This is the reason he chose the cross.

And you, being dead in your sins and the uncir-
cumcision of your flesh, hath he quickened
together with him, having forgiven you all tres-
passes; blotting out the handwriting of ordinances that was against us, which was contrary
to us, and took it out of the way, nailing it to his
cross; and having spoiled principalities and
powers, he made a shew of them openly, tri-
umphing over them in it. (Colossians
2:13-15 KJV)

Your Boaz is no joke.
He is willing to go the extra
mile for you. You are worth
it. Come on, bounce back
home. Don't keep your
Boaz waiting.

Your Boaz is no
joke. He is willing
to go the extra
mile for you. You
are worth it.

CHAPTER 6

"Will Thou Be Made Whole?"

Healing doesn't mean the damage never existed. It means the damage no longer controls our lives.[21]
Unknown Author

M Y BODY ACHES. My throat hurts. I don't feel good. I'm going to lay down here for a minute. Sound familiar? For most of us, the thought alone of being sick drives us bananas. Why? Because being sick, forces us to put all plans on hold, it restricts us from any advances as our bodies are unable to function as expected until we have fully recovered. Have you ever received a notice that you were going to be out sick on a specific date? When was the last time you received a text, email, or telegram that on the following weekend you would be bed bound because sickness was coming to visit? Probably never, right?

Sickness doesn't announce itself. It just arrives. Often, when you least expect it. So, what do you do when you are under the weather? Where do you go? Usually, prior to getting sick, our body sends us signs that something isn't right. Whether you choose to ignore the signs or not, how to proceed will be up to you. Ignoring it, doesn't make it go away. It's still there. And sooner or later you will have to face it.

You would think and assume that everybody wants to be healed, but to my surprise, I've come across many people who enjoy being sick. They use their sickness as a means to gain attention from those around them. On the other hand, those who have chosen not to ignore the signs, react by either:

1. **Visiting the nearest Pharmacy store**: They will stack up on all kinds of over the counter medication that will counteract and prevent the sickness from taking over.
2. **Home remedies**: You'll find that they will follow any home remedies methods in order to fight

against any sickness that wants to keep them bed bound.

3. **Primary Care Physician**: As a last resort, when our bodies do not respond to our quick solutions, a visit to our primary care physician will help with a more concrete diagnosis followed by a prescription that will effectively alleviate the condition in which we find ourselves.

Sickness is defined and generalized as the state of being ill. It's a disordered, weakened, or unsound condition. It could also mean a specific disease.[22] During biblical times, there were significant people who suffered different types of sickness, which are described as barrenness, blindness, leprosy, lame, paralytics, issue of blood flow and so on. Additionally, in the eyes of the religious leaders of Jesus' time, these people were considered as unclean, therefore, they weren't allowed to enter the Temple, the place where they believe God dwelled. Despite the reason for the illness, since some were born sick while others developed it later on, they sought for a solution as they didn't want to die in that condition.

Think about the lepers and the woman with the issue of blood for a minute. Both were considered unclean according to the law and religious leaders. The leper would become an outcast, as its condition was highly contagious.

They were forced to move out of their home and away from their loved ones and seclude themselves outside the city until they became better. They could not have any contact with other human beings. Once they were better, before returning home they needed to present themselves to the priest who then would give the final word (Leviticus 13:1-59). The condition of the woman with the issue of blood was seen as that of the leper. Although she wasn't forced to leave the comfort of her home, she couldn't touch no one or allow anyone to touch her. Religion condemned her to perpetual sterility. She found herself like many lepers during the time of Jesus' ministry between a rock and a hard place.

Do I continue to obey the Law? If I do, then of course, I will not sin but surely, I will die. However, if I break the law, I will have hope to live. Let me explain. They both were living. They would wake up every day, inhale and exhale the breath of life, eat, etc., but to enjoy life as intended, they couldn't. This is what they wanted, to enjoy life with no ailment as the Lord intended.

In the book of John, we find an interesting story of a nameless man who had been sick for thirty-eight years (John 5). That's a long time. Too long if you ask me. It's three to five days when we get the flu and we can't wait to recover, imagine thirty-eight years. Thirty-eight years is almost four decades. A lot happens in one year, let alone in thirty-eight. At first glance, we are not told the exact disease nor the cause for this man's illness, but the event indicates that it hindered his's ability to move and walk. However, later in the chapter Jesus finds him again. This time he is at the temple, and He tells him two interesting things (which we'll discuss later on) that alludes to the reason of his infirmity (John 5:14).

John lets us know about a place in Jerusalem, where the sick gathered by the masses in hopes to receive healing. This place in Hebrew was called Bethesda which means "house of mercy" or "house of grace." Also, in Hebrew and Aramaic Beth hesda could also mean "shame" or "disgrace." The meaning of this place is quite interesting, because although they weren't able to enter the Temple or attend any of the yearly festivals appointed by God due to their condition, the Lord in his infinite mercy provided a place where they could receive healing. The same place where they had to deal with shame and disgrace ended up being the same place where grace and mercy would be bestowed upon them. Additionally, they were surrounded by five porches. Five is the representation of grace. Grace is known to be the unmerited mercy that God gave to humanity by sending his son, Jesus Christ (John 3:16). It is by the grace of God, through His son Jesus who took upon Him all the sickness you and I would experience—physically, spiritually, and emotionally—that we may be made whole (Isaiah 53:1-5). We are not given any specifications as to how those with different illness arrived at the pool of Bethesda, however we do know that as they gathered, they were vigilant for that moment. They did not want to spend any more time than they had too there. John states that angel from time to time would trouble the waters and whomever was the first to step into the waters would be healed.

In essence, what drove them there to wait the move of the waters, was the need and desire to bounce back. What is your need or desire? Are you stuck? Are you sick today? Is there something that has stopped working, like your willingness to love and forgive or your mind and heart's attitude towards life? I don't know what their lives looked like before the illness, but I'm pretty sure it was better than where they were. But to be at that place was an indication that they were willing to do whatever it took as long as they were able to bounce back. John describes the sick or disabled people that would gather in Jerusalem, at the pool of Bethesda as (John 5:3 NIV): *the blind, the lame, and the paralyzed*. Now, John not only takes the time to let its reader know the amount of time this man had been

> Your position speaks louder than your words.

there. He also points out the position in which this man was in especially when Jesus saw him. This lets me know that your position matters. Your position speaks louder than your words.

Jesus makes a slight interruption to his itinerary and heads over to this man and asks him a rather unusual question—Will thou be made whole? (John 5:6) What kind of question is that? I could imagine the man's reaction and his inner conversation was something like this (*Seriously! Of course, I do. Isn't that why I am here?*). Well, just because you are in the right place doesn't mean that you want what it has to offer. You can go to the doctor's office, pay the co-pay, be examined, get your prescription filled and still not take it. Jesus' question wasn't to offend the man or to be sarcastic. His question was a rhetorical one. Rhetorical questions aren't meant to be answered. In fact, they are to cause a reaction that would prompt a change. In other words, Jesus' question was meant to cause him to think of the following: Why am I here? Why has it taken me this long to be whole? The man had no clue who he was talking to.

In his response, he starts to list the reasons why he is still in that same place. We call this today, excuses. Wouldn't you agree? How many excuses have you used to justify your condition? I know it's in our nature to find someone to blame. We learned it from Adam, when he blamed the woman God had given him as a help mate. It's always hard to take accountability for our own actions. Just because Jesus doesn't interrupt your excuses doesn't mean he is validating them. Stop attempting to justify the reasons you find yourself in the same position and ailment. It's time to bounce back. You are needed. Now, take a look at what Jesus does for this man. He removes the impossibility by telling him to do the following three specific things: rise up, pick up your mat and walk.

- **_Rise up_**: Notice that Jesus didn't help him to get up. Nor did he help him to the pool. He told him to "Rise Up." Jesus wanted this man to know, that he was greater than the angel who troubled the water from time to time. That he was the living word and that there is nothing like it. The centurion in Matthew 8:8 (emphasis added) told Jesus *"speak the word only, and my servant shall be healed."* That was enough for him and his servant back home who was sick of palsy and grievously tormented. He understood the power and authority wrapped in a word and in this case a word from Jesus. This wasn't any word. This was the living and active word (Hebrews 4:12), that no wall, no barriers, or fortress can hinder from doing that which it was been sent to do (Isaiah 55:11).

We often tend to depend and lean on others, but Jesus lets us know through this story that we have the ability to do it on our own. Lift yourself up. You got this and you can do it. Yes, I know it's been a while since you've done it on your own. But come on, you can do it. Put one foot in front of the other. Unlike the centurion, who needed a word, we find another man whose name is Jairus, in need of Jesus' hands. Jairus had a twelve-year-old daughter who was dying. He sought for the man who not only had a word, but whose hands were powerful enough to release the healing his daughter so much needed. Jesus accepts Jairus invitation to go to his house. Let me tell you that whenever Jesus accepts an invitation, get ready for something extraordinary to happen. As they begin to walk towards Jairus home, the writer in Mark 5 makes an interruption to highlight two things that happened:

1. He lets us know that Jesus was touched by a woman who had been suffering a blood flow for twelve years. As this woman touched Jesus, she was healed instantly and left to testify publicly of the transaction that had occurred in that moment. Why? Jairus, needed to build his faith for what he was about to witness once they arrived home (Mark 5:25-33).

2. He lets us know that as this woman was healed, Jairus receives news that his daughter has died. Before Jairus could say a word, Jesus looked

over to him and said, "Be not afraid, only believe" (Mark 5:34-36).

After this interruption, Jesus continues his journey to Jairus home, to fulfill the request made by him regarding his daughter. When they arrived, the house was full of commotion because the latest news was that the girl had died. Yet, when Jesus comes in, His report is different. He says, "The damsel is not dead, but sleepeth." When Jesus enters the room where the little girl was placed, he speaks a word to her "Talitha Cumi," which means "Damsel, I say unto thee, arise." The girl who for many was dead, exits the room alive, leaving everyone astonished. This is good to know, because it isn't over until HE says it is. Don't call it quits on your marriage, family, career, situation because of what it looks like on the surface. Jairus wanted Jesus to lay his hand on her, but Jesus gave something more powerful – *HIS WORD*. Jesus removed the impossibility, it's your turn to rise up now. His word is the sign that you can do it. Rise up!

- ***Pick up your mat***: The mat was the only piece of possession the sick had left besides the clothes on their back. They couldn't imagine their world without it. On this mat he spent his time sleeping, resting, and watching the world pass by. That's right, his world was at a standstill, while those around him kept moving by. Imagine the feelings of anger, frustration, disappointment, depression he battled alone on this mat. The countless nights he'd fallen asleep with tears dripping from his eyes at the thought of what could of or what should have been. Yet, on one particular day, one that he least expected, a man approaches him with a challenge he hasn't done before. Pick up your mat! Wait a minute. You want me to what? That would be our immediate reaction if we could be honest with ourselves. You are asking me to interrupt the relationship I have with my mat for what exactly?

What most of us fail to understand and comprehend at the moment, which I'm sure this man didn't too, is that the mat that was serving him rest, comfort and security was actually keeping him hostage. I don't know what your mat is or what it looks like. But the mat is the thing that you turn to when all else fails or stops working. It could be your money, job, health, friends, stores, bad habits, excessive spending, and so on. Jesus arrived at the precise moment, to let this man know that God's plan for his life was far greater than what he could imagine. It was going to require that He let go of what seemed comfortable and secure at the moment to embrace the new that was to come.

111

Today, my friend, hear the voice of God through the Holy Spirit telling to pick up your mat. Stop laying in it. You no longer need that mat as you think. Jesus is your rock, comfort, fortress, high tower, resting place. Jesus is our hope when all else fails. Jesus is our way when we feel lost. Jesus is the answer when all else seems contrary. Notice that He didn't tell him to get rid of the mat. He only instructed him to pick it up. Let your mat serve now as a testimony that what you held one day so tightly, now points to the hope you have in Christ. Don't lay back in your mat, pick it up and witness to the world around you that the same God who did it for this man, has done it again with you. Don't get tired of carrying your mat, get tire of sleeping in it and seeing the world pass by in it. Trust that the one who bid you to walk is the same one that will provide and comfort for you now. Stop laying on the mat when he has told you to pick it up. Yes, it's going to require faith and faith comes by hearing the word of God. The word of God is that all you need to bounce back is in Christ. Depend on Him and His strength (Ephesians 6:10).

- **_Walk_**: If you thought that the rise up and pick up your mat command was challenging, then think again. Walking requires an action, not just merely a thought or spoken word. Walking involves the assurance that as I act upon the driving force in my mind (thought or desire), the action taken will led to the destination in mind. Sadly, here is where most people often decide to settle where they are at and quit on every effort to move forward. Due to the uncertainty of what will happen, they much rather stay within the familiarity, despite what it may look like. Listen, faith is given to all.

However, not all takes the time to cultivate it and allow it to grow. There are no limits in faith. Faith is attracted to hopeless situation. Faith isn't afraid of people's thoughts, and definitely doesn't go into a crisis when it senses unbelief in the atmosphere. Nevertheless, faith is sure of what its performing abilities are. Hebrews tells us that faith is the assurance of that which is not seen (Hebrews 11:1). Yet, James states that in order for faith to work it needs to be accompanied by action (James 2:14-17). It is why I believe the apostle Paul lets us know in 2 Corinthians 5:7 that we walk by faith and not by sight. Stop looking at your condition and start walking. Dan Kitz stated in his article *"Pick up your mat and walk"* that walking into spiritual wholeness means that we leave our mats behind and move from our identification with what put us there, into an identification of who we are in Christ. We learn to submit ourselves to the work of the Holy Spirit and walk with our brothers

113

and sisters into the challenges that the Lord equips us to fulfill.[23]

Healing is a progressive process. As we continue to walk, following the orders given from above, we will be transformed into that which he has destined us to be. I won't lie. There will be times that we may feel as if nothing is changing or happening but trust me there is something taking place. You may not see it but those around you do. So, don't stop walking. Take a look at two of favorite accounts in The Bible:

1. **Mephibosheth (2 Samuel 4):** Mephibosheth, who at the age of five years old, suffered a terrible accident at the expense of his caregivers' fear. The accident left him crippled and destitute in a place called Lo-debar. Lo-debar was known as the land of "no pasture," "no word," or "no communication." In other words, whoever dwells there was forgotten. Yet, we see, that in this same place, Mephibosheth is called to the Kings palace. It is in Lo-debar, where Mephibosheth is shown grace and favor. The King had sent for him. When King gives an order, it doesn't matter where you find yourself, you will be found. You may not have Wi-Fi,

internet, phone, computer, or any other electronic devices used for communication, but if the King has summons you, you will be found. Mephibosheth was crippled and lame by the hand of one, yet by the hand of another he is blessed and position at king's table. The beauty of it all is knowing that although we have no records that he ever physically walked, we are shown a vivid picture of what took place at the Kings table. He may have felt as the same man who left Lo-debar, but at the table he wasn't knows as a lame crippled nobody who had come from Lo-debar. He was knowns at the man whom the king decided to bless. What other saw as they looked at Mephibosheth, was a display of what grace, mercy, and favor looked like. His shortcomings, deficiencies and disabilities were all covered at the king's table.

2. **Lame man at the gate of the Temple "Beautiful" (Acts 3):** On the other hand, you have a man who was born lame. He's taken daily to lay at the gate of the Temple to beg. He's taken to the place he should have access to but because of his condition he can't. Do you know what it is to see people day after day or year

after year, come and go, yet you are in the same place? Yet, it's here, at the gate of the Temple called "Beautiful," where this man receives an unexpected life altering miracle. He is used to asking for money, yet what Peter and John gives him, money can't buy. The lame man is challenged to do what he has never done in his life. Peter tells him "Rise up and Walk." The writer lets us know that the lame man indeed leaps up, walks, and praises God as he enters the Temple with Peter and John. What catches my attention is that the people saw him walking and praising. Why couldn't they see the leap? The leaping is your reminder of what has been done, is taking place and what will happen for you. I know this is hard to comprehend because we want to feel different or see ourselves different before acting out in faith.

Listen, if you can see yourself healed, whole, walking, loving, forgiving, and trying again, then guess what, you can do it. Start leaping into your new walk. Don't be like Peter who was bid to walk and became distracted and began to sink (Matthew 14:22-33). Remain focus on the one who told you to walk, for he is the author and finisher of our faith (Hebrew 12:2). Will you today, respond to the calling of the King like Mephibosheth? Or will you dare to be challenged and leap your way into what you've been called?

This is a call to action, which means having faith and trust in God while getting rid of every dead weight and hindrances that are besetting us and preventing us from walking and embracing God's gifts and calling for us (Hebrews 12:1). What would you do differently if Jesus removed the impossibility set before you today? Would you be brave enough to stand? How about to walk? What about to talk?

> What would you do differently if Jesus removed the impossibility set before you today?

The barrier is moved so that you can accomplish that which you were created and destined for. Almost every encounter Jesus had with those being healed, after the miracle, He would tell them either your sins are forgiven, or your faith has saved you. Yet, when this man is made whole, there isn't anything Jesus says afterwards. However, we do read later in that chapter that Jesus finds this man again at the temple (V. 14) and tells him:

1. *See that you have been made whole (healed)*: If you remember, the only question Jesus asked the man was

117

if he wanted to be whole? He didn't ask what had happened to him? What did he do or didn't do? That really didn't matter. Jesus gave him what he needed, a second chance in life. He restored him completely. That's the beauty about Jesus. He doesn't do half through jobs. What he starts, he finishes. If he's going to heal you, it's going to be done completely not halfway. If he's going to break the chains, he's going to do it all the way and not some. He made the man whole again. Whole physically, emotionally, and spiritually.

2. *Sin no more*: This statement and declaration, let us know that the reason the man had spent thirty-eight years in the same condition, unable to move or walk, had to do with sin. Not every sickness has to do with sin, but it's evident that sin plays a huge part. During this timeframe, it was believed that those experiencing such sickness was a result of sin. It is why Jesus' disciples asked him upon meeting a man who was born blind in John 9:2, who sinned, this man or his parents? His sickness was so that God would be glorified. But as we study this particular case, Jesus tells him to "Sin no more." Why? Because sin brings destruction. Paul said in Romans 6:23,

"For the wages of sin is death, but the gift of God
is eternal life through Jesus Christ our Lord."

Sin equals death. It's not a physical death, but a spiritual
death. This death causes a separation between us and
God. If there is anything you and I will need in this life,
is the connection to God. What connects us to God is
a sin free life. You might be asking yourself, "How can
I live a sinless life?" I'm glad you asked. Clearly, we are
unable to live a sinless life, due to the sinful nature we
acquired from Adam. We were conceived and born into
sin according to David (Psalm 51:5). Yet, through Jesus
Christ, who paid the price to deal with sin, we can try to
make our lives this sinless life by refusing to give in to its
lure. Also, when we fall short, Jesus has provided a way
to restore us back, as long as we confess the wrongdoing
and receive his forgiveness in return (1 John 1:9). Sin,
no matter it's degree, will cause you to miss the mark.
Don't fall prey to its lust of the flesh, lust of the eyes
and pride of life (1 John 2:16). Jesus wanted this man
to know and understand the issue with sin. Sin looks
good for a moment, but its effect is detrimental. It's not
that I (Jesus) can't do it again (heal, make you whole,
forgive you) but remember where I took you out from.
Don't forget how "*sin*" trapped you in a place, unable
to move or walk for thirty-eight years.

Just as Jesus had removed the barrier, or impossibility this man faced to bounce back, He has done for us through his death and resurrection. Please take a moment to read Ephesians 2:1-22. One day, you and I were dead in our transgression and sin, but God, who loved us, gave His only begotten son, so that we could be quicken together with Christ, risen together with Him and made us sit together in Heavenly places. Do you know how many people today find themselves just like this man at the pool of Bethesda? They are physically well, with bodily movements intact, however, emotionally, and spiritually they are paralyzed. When you look from the outside in, they seem to have it going well. Nice car, home, great job, steady income, terrific family and so on. But when you take a look from the inside out, they are stuck, unable to move forward in life emotionally and spiritually.

Often, the main cause of their emotional or spiritual paralysis is due to traumatic events experienced in their life. Events that have left them immobile to feel, react and enjoy life. Afraid to try. Afraid to laugh. Afraid to trust. Trauma is a severe shock and pain caused by an extreme upsetting experience. Traumas could range from all sorts of categories, such as rape, molestation, betrayal, domestic violence, adultery, loss of loved ones, car accident, and so on. Each trauma, no matter at what age, impacts the individual differently. Years can pass and everything around you can change with time, but due to the trauma experienced, you continue to feel its aftermath constantly. In a nutshell, trauma refers to wounding. When you have been wounded, it affects your psyche in many ways.

It is with this particular thing or feeling that Jesus wants to heal and make whole again. He wants you to know that you can stay with the memory of the event but let me take away the pain that continues to shock you every time you remember the trauma. He wants us to be whole in every area of our life. God calls us to healing and in fact, he wants to heal us. Healing is not a magical wand. It's a process that takes time. Healing doesn't mean you forget the event, but that you get past the hurt. The most important and initial step in regaining your emotional and spiritual agility is to accurately diagnose the nature of what ails you.

I found myself like this man at the pool of Bethesda, the only difference is that instead of being there thirty-eight years, I spent ten. Ten years nurturing my illness of bitterness. I wanted to be whole but just as the man at the pool, I kept justifying the reason I was there. My bitterness was a result of betrayal. This traumatic event left me scarred and sent me into a despair that really, I didn't see any way out. The more I thought about it and concentrated on the trauma, the more it ate away at my mind, clouding all reasoning and desire of getting whole. I would roll out my mat and lay in it as I'd nurture my pain day in and day out.

It wasn't until I took the medication found in the word that would heal and restore me back, that I started to feel better. The medication was called forgiveness. When I began to forgive, I started to feel relief, but the full relief came when I forgave myself. That's right! I needed to forgive myself. It was here that true healing and wholeness took place. By choosing to justify my condition along with the hurt and pain others had caused me, I was allowing sin to destroy my purpose in life. How? By not forgiving the offense. The Bible tells us clearly to forgive in order to be forgiven. Forgiveness isn't an option, it's a commandment. Forgiveness is an intentional and voluntary process to release the feeling of resentment or vengeance towards the offender. When I finally decided to respond to the challenge set before – rise up, pick up your mat and walk—I remember like yesterday how my life began to change.

> Forgiveness isn't an option, it's a commandment.

My hardest part was learning how to walk in the healing he had provided for me. For me I still felt the betrayal, anger, and resentment yet, I had to push through knowing that he had delivered me from my infirmity of bitterness. That wasn't easy, as it challenged my faith, but today, I can say without a shadow of doubt, that I've experienced what Joel 2:25 declares:

"And I will restore to you the years that the locust hath eaten, the cankerworm, and the caterpillar, and the palmerworm, my great army which I sent among you."

It's without a doubt that trauma changes you but by the same token, healing also changes you. How many years have you allowed the illness of "Bitterness, resentment, and hate" weaken your ability to forgive? How many years have you allowed the illness of "lust, envy, and malice" to eat away your sight? How many years have you allowed the illness of "lie" to eat the fruit of your lips?

> It's without a doubt that trauma changes you but by the same token, healing also changes you.

I don't know where you find yourself today, but I invite you to the place where Hannah entered to deal with the illness in her heart. How long she suffered, I don't know. How long she went up to Shiloh and back home the same way she entered the temple, I don't know. But this I do know, is that on this one particular day she went up a mess but came down transformed (1 Samuel 1:1-21). She broke the silence. It's time to bounce back. Jesus has made the way for you. All you have to do, is rise up, pick up your mat and walk. If Leah, Naomi, Hannah, and this man could bounce back, so can you.

Conclusion

Birth Your
Judah Praise

CHAPTER 7

The Power and Effect of Praise

When you enter God's presence with praise,
He enters your circumstances with power.[24] –
Unknown Author

TESTING, TESTING. TESTING one, two. Testing.
One, two, three. Got it. This is usually what we hear
when someone is performing a test check on something,
like the sound of a microphone. Sometimes, they'll even
give the microphone love taps with two fingers, then speak

into it "testing, one-two." In a similar manner, I would like to invite you to do a "sound check" on yourself today. Yes, I know that sounds crazy, but work with me. Take two fingers and place them on your wrist of the opposite hand. Do you have a pulse? Great. Now, pass your hand over your nose. Do you feel the air exhaling from your nose? Awesome. Do you know what that means? You are alive. You may not have much. In fact, you probably don't have much to look forward to this day, but the matter of the fact is, that you are ALIVE.

Have you ever wondered; how many people did not have the chance to wake up today? But you did! Not because you did anything for it, or how healthy you think you are; you woke up today because God decided to renew His mercy over your life (Lamentation 3:22-23). Guess what? He didn't have to do it. But he did. He did it, despite the mess you may find yourself in. He did it in spite of the challenges you may be facing today. He did it because of His love, mercy, and faithfulness in spite of our transgressions and unfaithfulness. Did you know that we all have more than one reason to sing a praise of thanksgiving to the Lord? Why? For all he has done for us. That's right, he has done more for us than any other on this earth. He's provided for us, like the rain, the sun, the food we eat, the clothes we dress, the house we live in, the car we drive and the job we have. He takes care of us while we sleep, while on the road, in school, at work, or even at the grocery store. He forgave and He forgives our sins, the ones we commit daily, both consciously and unconsciously. Should I go one? This and many more reasons like this should cause us to send the Lord a praise.

When was the last time you praised the Lord? I'm not just saying a simple Hallelujah or Glory to God praise. I'm talking about a praise that comes from the depths of your soul, as if it's your last breath and you want it to be a praise to God. What motivates you or ignites a passion in you to praise God? Do you praise Him because of what He has done for you or because of who He is? Do you praise Him when things are going well, or do you know how to praise Him when things are upside down and going terribly wrong too? I know it's easier to praise when things are going well and when God has come through for you. I've been there and done that. Moses' sister has been there too.

In the book of Exodus, we see how Miriam broke out with tambourines, shouts, and praises as she had reached the other side and saw how the Egyptians were being swallowed up by the same waters that had parted ways for them all to cross over (Exodus 15:20-21). But are you able to praise Him in advance? Before seeing it happen, like the breakthrough, the healing, the promotion, the ministry, or your deliverance. How is His credit with you? Has He ever failed you? I'm guessing not, right? You need to know that

God does not suffer from a lack of self-esteem. That He needs you to praise Him to feel like God. In fact, the book of Revelation tells us that He is surrounded by angels, twenty-four elders, and four weird looking beasts who praise and worship Him all day long (Revelation 4:1-11). Yet, there is one praise that he longs to hear. That is your praise. My praise. The redeemed praise. There is no praise like the one that comes from a thankful heart. One that recognizes that if it had not been for the Lord. Go ahead, take a minute (sixty seconds) to praise Him for His goodness and mercy. I'll wait. In fact, I'll join you.

I'm sure you are quite familiar with David and how he loved to praise the Lord. David wrote something that for many years boggled my mind. It's found in Psalms 34:1 and says:

> "I will bless the Lord at all times: his praise shall continually be in my mouth."

I always wondered what David could have possibly be thinking when he said, "all times" and "continually." Does he not know how hard it is to praise God when you've had a rough day? When you've learned that the one you've vowed to be with 'til death do you apart has left you to be in the arms of someone else? Or when your child who is supposed to be your sweet little angel overnight turns on you with no explanation whatsoever? However, "all times" means in the good as well as the bad times. I know it's easier to praise in the good times. When everything is going handy dandy. But most of us struggle with praising the Lord in the bad times. We seem to pick up Job's wife's attitude. For many years, I struggled with the concept of praise. I would see how others who were going through rough patches would gather at church and praise God as if nothing was wrong.

I couldn't. For me, I view this as being a hypocrite and I wasn't going to be one. I wasn't going to pretend that everything was ok, when down deep inside I was a mess. I didn't mind going to church on a rough day, but you wouldn't catch me opening my mouth to give God the praise He deserved in spite of my "rough day." See, my so called "rough day" could've consist of either my kids driving me crazy, my husband doing something I didn't like or someone cutting me off while driving. Little things like this that now in retrospect were so insignificant yet got the best of me. It wasn't until I truly learned that my praise to God didn't depend on a good or bad day I could of have, but on his goodness.

David said, "His" praise. Whose praise? God's praise. That meant that it belonged to God although it was on David's lips. He couldn't remain quiet. Regardless of the situation he may be

> Praise is the channel in which we communicate with God.

131

facing, he needed to praise God. He found connection, peace, security, refuge, strength, deliverance, and wisdom through praise. Praise is the channel in which we communicate with God. Having a little more knowledge today, I know what David meant by "all times" and continually." He was vocally expressing his lifetime commitment with God, which he held himself accountable as seen in Psalms 42:5 when he said:

> "Why art thou cast down, O my soul? And why
> art thou disquieted in me? Hope thou in God:
> for I shall yet praise him for the help of his
> countenance."

He knew the secret behind a praise not only by his life experiences, but also by its origins. Have you ever heard about the "law of first mention?" The law of first mention means that the first time a word occurs in Scriptures gives the key to understand its meaning in every other place.[25]" Did you know when was the first time "praise" was mentioned in The Bible? It is first mentioned in Genesis by a woman named Leah, the mother of Judah who was the ancestor of King David according to the New Testament genealogy account of Jesus. That's right, praise is introduced by a woman who teaches us the power and effect of a praise in the midst of her darkest situation. Let's examine the below encounters with praise.

- **Leah: <u>The Cycle Breaker Praise</u>**

Leah was the first to experience the power and effect praise has in the life a person. Her praise was birth out of pain. Pain that had been caused by betrayal, rejection, abandonment, and despair. Pain can either bring out the best or worse in a person. In life, we all deal with pain, one way or another. Pain can be experienced either physically –like being cut, labor and delivery, surgery— or emotionally –like an offense by a word or action. However, every pain at any level –moderate to excru-ciating—can be managed. Pain is a feeling, and feeling can be managed. We can go to the hospital for the same condition and the doctor will ask us both to number our pain from a scale of one to ten. What can be a two for me might be an eight for someone else or what can be a three for you can be a ten for me. Even though we all handle pain differently, pain can be managed.

Leah who had been hurt emotionally, allowed pain to create repetitive cycles in her life. She got tired anes-thetizing the pain. One day, she decided to deal with the pain differently. She took the pain and made an exchange. She traded her ashes for beauty, mourning for the oil of joy and the spirit of heaviness for the garment of praise (Isaiah 61:3). Did you understand that? She traded that which held her down and out, for a layer of garment that refreshed her soul. A garment in fact is something that must be put on.

You must make a decision and then take action to put the "garment" on. It's not going to hop on to you. You don't stand in front of your closet and tell your clothes to dress you, right? You have to pick them out, and then place them on one by one. The garment of praise works the same way. You have to take off the weight of failure, depression, loneliness, sorrow and put on the garment of praise. This garment is light and comfortable. How long are you going to carry with the spirit of heaviness? It's called heaviness for a reason. The Hebrew word for heaviness is *keheh*, which means "dim, dull, or faint." The ultimate goal of this spirit of heaviness is to keep you bound in pain, stuck and confine to a lifestyle that was not created for you. How long will you allow the pain of your situation control your life? Time is short and should be used efficiently and effectively. Your life has an expiration date, and how sad would it be that you were unable to live it to the fullest because of your inability to deal with your pain. Forgive me please, as it's not my intent to minimize or take lightly the pain you've experienced in live or dismiss the situation that you are going through now.

In fact, I want you to know that I as Leah had to take a step back and weigh my options. Is it all worth it? To trust God. Is He going to treat me like others have? Is he going to fail? Will he be able to provide my needs? I needed to decide to let go and let God take control. I had to pack pains suitcase and tell her it was time to go, that she had overstayed her welcome. I took charge of my life, my feelings and emotions and began to release what was stored deep inside me—a Judah praise.

Leah gave birth to more than just a son, she birthed a cycle breaker. Judah, who name means "Praise" or "let Jehovah be praised," brought her from obscurity to marvelous light. It broke every cycle and tendency she needed of validation—to be seen, heard, and joined— from men right into the presence of God, where she found fulfillment. Although there is no record found in scriptures that her situation changed as the results of "praise," yet, we do know that she was a changed and transformed into another woman.

- **Tamar (Genesis 38): <u>Breakthrough Praise</u>**

Have you ever heard of Tamar? Do you know where she comes from? Who her family is? I don't either, but what I do know, is that when I grow up, I want to be like her. To be bold, strong, and fearless in the midst of opposition. She taught me to provoke change. Yes, I know that she is often criticized and harshly judged by what she did, but when taken the time to understand her actions in context, you'll soon discover that anyone in her shoes would have done the same thing.

For some, she will forever be reminded as the one who was bold enough to do the unthinkable in order to receive that which she knew she could produce. She's a woman who provoked such change that brought about the breakthrough she desperately needed. Tamar's connection with praise came from experiencing pain, disappointments, and humiliation. She had become a widow not once, but twice, in fact a childless widow and then was sent home empty handed to wait until the last son, whose name was Shelah, was ready to be given unto marriage.

She's first introduced as the one chosen to be a wife for one of Judah's son, Er. What specific traits, qualities or characteristics Tamar had, that Judah would take her instead of another? We don't know. Yet, she was the one chosen to for the task. Did he really pick her, or did God have something to do with this? Solomon states the following in Proverbs 16:1, 33:

> The preparations of the heart in man, and the answer of the tongue, is from the Lord.

> The lot is cast into the lap; but the whole disposing thereof is of the Lord.

So, what is it to be chosen after all? It's to be hand selected amongst many. To be observed, studied, and found adequately capable for the task. Think about a puzzle. How many pieces have you ever tried to fit into a place to then find that it doesn't belong there? No matter how much you try and how good it may look, it doesn't fit. Why? Because there is one piece that was shaped specifically for that location.

Many may look like the right piece of puzzle for that job, calling, career, assignment, yet you have been chosen for it. You have what it takes for the task. Often, when we are chosen, we don't feel adequate for the task. We believe and most convince themselves that they are the wrong selection but let me remind you of something vitally important "God makes no mistake when he chooses someone." Take a look at a few cases found in scriptures of those who were hand selected by God, who did not feel adequate for the task, yet were the missing piece needed for such a time as that:

- **Moses (Exodus 3-4)**: When called and chosen by God, Moses was out living in Midian as a fugitive. When God gave him the rundown of the task, he told God that his brother Aaron was a better fit for the task because he was slow of speech and tongue. I love God's response to Moses in the next verse: Who gave human beings their mouths? Who makes them deaf or mute? Who gives them sight or makes them blind? Is it not I, the Lord? Now go; I will help you speak and will teach you what to say. Despite all of God's comebacks, Moses still bid the Lord to send someone else for the task. Did God listen to Moses? Absolutely not. God still did it with Moses, because although Aaron seemed like the right fit in Moses' eyes, to God he wasn't. God had other plans with Aaron.

- **Deborah (Judges 4:1-5:31)**: She could had been born at any other time, but God sent her for such a time during the period of Judges. She was the only woman mentioned to be a leader during this timeframe. She was a brave and courageous woman who did not allow their enemy at the time, Sisera who had nine hundred chariots of iron, to intimidate her. She rose up like a mother over her nation. She fought for peace, liberty, and justice. She led the army with Barak and victory was received and the land once again rested for forty years.

- **Jeremiah (Jeremiah 1:5):** When called by God as a prophet the first and only thing he told God was that he was a kid. God wasn't too concerned with that. All he knew was that Jeremiah was the man for the hour. He had been known, sanctified, and ordained as such by God way before he was born. Of course, God could have chosen others, yet, they didn't have the cut or design Jeremiah did for the task. Jeremiah had the heart to submit and obey to the Lords commands and serve as a mouthpiece on behalf of the Lord without altering the prophetic message.

- **Mary (mother of Jesus) (Luke 1:26-38):** She was engaged to Joseph when visited by Angel Gabriel, who notified her that she had been chosen to birth the Son of God. In her response we know that she didn't feel worthy enough for such task but grateful and thankful to have been selected.

- **Paul (1 Corinthians 15:1-10):** Chosen way before his encounter with Jesus. He is first known as Saul, who used to kill Christian Jews who would profess Jesus as their Lord and Savior. Today, we are so thankful and grateful that Paul opened his heart to the Lord and underwent a complete transformation, as one third of the New Testament books are written by him. God even gave testimony about Paul's new identity in Christ when He summoned Ananias to inquire about him in the house of Judas (Acts 9:10-19). People were afraid of him because of the reputation he had, yet, when he had an encounter with Jesus his life was changed forever.

- **Esther (Esther 4:13-17):** Mordecai needed to remind Esther that for such a time as the one they were living she had been chosen to become Queen. Passed the glamour, royal clothing and servants laid an intercessor who would advocate for the people of God. She would had never thought in a million years that an orphan like her would one day become a Queen. She was the woman of the hour who God appointed for such task. She did not let anything stand in her way to deliver God's people in time of need.

However, before Tamar and Er were able to start a family, his days are shortened. She is now given unto

Onan, who has no problem fulfilling the levirate law (Deut. 25:5-10) yet refuses to impregnant her. Every intimate moment they had, instead of reaching the maximum level of intimacy, he would spill over on the ground. As if, it wasn't enough that she lost her first husband prematurely, she is now married to his brother who has no intention whatsoever to keep his brother's name alive and as a result, is left again as a childless widow. Can you imagine how humiliating and devastating this was for Tamar?

I know that for most woman today, this may not be much of an issue, at least with bearing a child. See, children for most are view as a hindrance with their agenda, career, and lifelong plans or with their figure. Nevertheless, children are a blessing from God, and nothing happens just by accident. The child may have not been planned in your calendar, but in Gods they were already penciled in. In fact, you would never know the blessings you'll reap from that child. Trust me. After I had my first child, I swore that I would not have any more children. The experience and pain from that pregnancy left me traumatized. When I found out that I was with child, I was lost both physically and emotionally. All my plans, projects and personal desires again were going to be placed on hold. Mind you, at the time I was barely twenty going on twenty-one. I did not want to bring another child into this world. For me, I wasn't ready. It wasn't what I wanted. But God had other plans. Plans that if he would had share with me at that time, I still would have said no.

The next couple of months were horrible, despite growing up in a home where abortion wasn't practiced or encouraged, and even knowing what the bible teaches about this topic, I looked for ways that I could provoke a miscarriage. I couldn't bear the thought of going through the traumatic event of delivery; while at the same time, my marriage wasn't as stable as I would have liked it to be. But on the day my child was scheduled to be born, as I was being prepared to undergo a caesarean delivery—the same process that had traumatized me a year ago— I felt a sense of unexplainable calm in my inner woman. As I entered into the delivery room, I noticed that the doctor who would be performing my c-section wasn't my regular Ob/Gyn. She had been called into another emergency case. When the whole process was done, the doctor looks over to us as he held our son in his hands, and asked us, "What will his name be?" and as if we had been rehearsing for this moment, we responded simultaneously and in one accord "Nathan." To which the doctor looked down at me and said, "What a gift you have been given." Little did I know that the meaning of his name in Hebrew meant "Gift of God."

This child has truly been a gift not only to me but to our entire family. There is never a dull moment whenever Nathan is around. Today, I'm so thankful for the gift the Lord saw fit for me, even when I couldn't see it then. This gift is a constant reminder to me of how God knows best and that he will wipe away every tear, take away every pain while comforting our hearts. Nevertheless, in the early biblical times, woman yearned, desired, cried, and pleaded with God for the chance and opportunity to bear a child. They believed that being barren was a curse by God (Job 15:34). Below is a list of women who had their wombs shut by God:

- **Sarah (Genesis 21:1-3)**: She is the wife of God's friend and the father of faith—*Abraham*. She is promised a child in her old age. She waited years for this promise and after her mistake of going before God's timing, she conceives Isaac as promised by God. Her womb was open in her old age. Gen. 21:1-3 (Isaac)

- **Rebekah (Genesis 25:21)**: She is the wife of the promised child, Isaac. She went twenty years waiting to conceive until she insisted her husband pray to God and inquire about her case. How long thereafter we don't know, but she conceived and bore not one son but two—Esau and Jacob.

- **Rachel (Genesis 30:22-24):** She is the woman Jacob feel head over heels for. He worked fourteen years for her because he loved her. After spending years enjoying the company of nephews and nieces, she please and asks for a child of her own. She became the mother of Joseph and Benjamin.

- **Manoah's wife (Judges 13:1-3):** Her name is not recorded in the pages of The Bible, yet, her sweet scent of humility and honor is smelled through this chapter as we read the intimate conversation between her and the angel of the Lord, who visited her not once but twice. What honor she must have felt to be chosen to bare a son, and raise him up un the Nazarite covenant for such specific task for God? It was so much that she didn't even ask the angel for his name. She becomes the mother of Samson, one of the nation's leaders during the one of the darkest periods of Israel.

- **Hannah (1 Samuel 1:19-20):** She is one of the two wives' brother Elkanah had, whom he loved even though she hadn't bore any children. His love for her wasn't predicated upon what she could give but on who she was and meant to him. However, it was a dream for every woman to become a mother. In Hannah's case, it's not that she was barren, but that God had shut up her womb for the moment. God's plans for Hannah were far greater than what she could had ever imagined. He did not want to just give her a son, He wanted to give the nation through her a prophet. After she prayed earnestly one day at Shiloh, she went back home to find that her womb was carrying a world changing son—*Samuel*. She went on to have five other children (1 Samuel 2:21).

- **Michal (2 Samuel 6:23):** She was one of the first wives David had. She was the daughter of King Saul and was given as a prize to David for defeating the giant who had defied the army of the Lord for forty days. Michal's bareness is sadly attributed to the attitude displayed when she saw her husband and King dancing before the Lord when the ark of the covenant had been brought to Jerusalem.

- **Elizabeth (Luke 1:13):** She is the wife of Zacharias, one of the of the priest who in her old age was granted the desire to have a child, John the Baptist. She praises the Lord for such miracle and declares that the Lord has taken away her reproach among men.

Children are a blessing from God (Psalm 127:3) and without the fruit of your womb, not only were you seen as a condemned sinner, but also a woman without purpose. In Tamar's case, she isn't mentioned to be barren. In fact, her name means "date" (the fruit), "date palm" or just "palm tree." In other words, she was fertile and ready to produce. Sadly, both connections to bearing a child had died prematurely by the hand of the Lord.

Judah decides that the best thing to do is to send Tamar home to wait until his last son is ready to be given unto marriage. Although there is no place like home, imagine the pain and shame that Tamar felt as she journeyed back home. Who knows all the sideline conversations, rumors and judgment she must have heard while heading back home, to await the one that would prove them all wrong and would break the affront that grew heavier each day over her? Nonetheless, she arrives home and begins her waiting period.

Having to wait is one of the hardest things we can be asked to do. No matter how patient a person can be, when you are asked to wait, and nothing seems to be happening, trust me that sooner or later you become irritable, impatient, and bothered. The bottom line of the matter is that nobody likes to wait. Even if the wait is on the Lord and his timing, we find ourselves struggling from time to time with this as well. Although we know and understand that God's timing is PERFECT. Now, it's another thing having to wait on men. OMG! Men always change their mind or has an excuse to justify the reason they haven't been able to fulfill their word. In Tamar's case, how long do you think she had to wait?

Unfortunately, we are not provided with the timeframe she spent waiting for Judah and Shelah's visit. Who knows all the questions that bombarded her mind as she waited? This is where waiting becomes difficult. You find yourself questioning God and His plans-questioning yourself too. You see that your outward situation or atmosphere does not match what is going on in the inside of you. What do you do when you know that you are ready for change, ready to seize the moment that's approaching but you are stuck waiting for that one missing link? Where do you go? Who do you turn to? How much longer do you wait? As she waited for Shelah, whose name means "to break," "that unties," or "that undresses" she wanted more than just someone who could break, untie, and undress the affront she carried for years. She wanted connection. Connection is defined as a relationship in which a person or thing is linked or associated with something else.[26] But when you find connection, what seemed impossible and unimaginable overpowers you in such way that there is no marching back.

My husband shared with me one day, an issue he had encountered at work. He was given the task to figure out why a ceiling lamp was not functioning properly. As he investigated the situation, he found that as he tested for power, he had power going to the lamp, but the lamp still wouldn't turn on. As he took another look, he realized that up in the attic was an electrical box that had a cross wire, causing the lamp its inability to function as expected. He explained that for power to run effectively through the wires, it needs both a negative and a positive. Having two positives will send you on an overload while having two negatives will leave you with no power at all.

As Tamar connected with Judah, she was able to experience the breakthrough she'd been waiting for such a long time. In this case, Tamar apparently had been connected twice to two negative poles (Er and Onan). However, when she dared to connect with Judah who represents "praise" she found that he was the positive pole. Her situation was negative as she had lost two husbands, had nothing really to give but brokenness, however, when she brought what she had and connected with "praise," he was able to do for her more than what she could had imagine. What are you connected to today? Where do you continue to draw your help from? Dare to connect with Praise today? The connection to praise will set you up for the breakthrough you need. Breakthrough refers to any significant or sudden advancement, development, achievement, or increase, as in scientific knowledge or diplomacy that removes a barrier to progress. Have you had quite enough of fail attempts? What sudden advancement are you in need of today? Are you willing to provoke a change? How do you want to be remembered? I urge you to connect today with praise. You will not regret it.

- **Paul & Silas (Acts 16:11-40):**
  The Midnight Hour Praise

Paul and Silas were two men chosen, separated, and appointed by God to preach the gospel of the good news of Jesus Christ. This was only a confirmation to Paul of that which the Lord had spoken to him when he had his encountered and transformation with Jesus many years before. There is nothing like the right time. The calling itself has nothing to do with our abilities, our talents, or our knowledge, rather it has all to do with the one who called us. When God calls someone for a specific task. He will equip them with what is needed both –spiritually and physically—in order to fulfill the call.

Jesus selected twelve ordinary men as disciples, who later would become apostles. When He rose from the dead and before ascending to Heaven, he'd given them the task known as "The Great Commission (Matthew 28:16-20)" but prior to fulfilling this task, they had to stay in Jerusalem until they had endued with power from on high (Luke 24:49; Acts 1). The waiting for this endowment was vitally important as it would give them with more than just an outer ward manifestation of the Holy Spirit. It would equip them inwardly, strengthening their inner man with all patience and longsuffering with joyfulness (Colossians 1:11), for the task on hand (John 14:26; 1 John 2:20-27).

On one of their missionary trips, as they had finished preaching, healing the sick and casting out demons, they were charged, beaten, and cast into prison. This was one of the many different types of affronts that the men and woman of God who had been called and appointed, had to endure as a good soldier of Jesus Christ (2 Timothy 2:3-4). After suffering such beating and left with unattended wounds, Paul and Silas decided to do something quite out of the ordinary. At midnight they break out with a song and praise to God in the midst of their affliction. That's right. They didn't wait until they were healed or free from jail. They praised right in the midst of the pain and suffering. In fact, they praised while their skins burned and bleed. This is something that nowadays we are not used to seeing or doing. We rather sit back and complain. It's not that we don't want to see God at work, of course we do, but not at our expense.

Let me tell you that Paul and Silas had every right to be angry, to be upset, to be in a bad mood, to complain and question God. The situation they were enduring was not fair and they were Roman citizens, yet, instead of opening their mouths in their own defense, they suffered it out together, singing and praising God during the midnight hour. Who said singing was only for church? Or you could only sing when the choir and musicians are around? Wherever there is a true worshiper, or someone with a grateful heart, they don't need to wait for the musicians or to be in a church, they will use their hands, their feet or whatever they have around to send a melodical praise to God.

What amazes me with this story is their choice to sing and praise instead of complaining. Whether or not they knew the effects of complaining or not, the fact that their first choice was to praise is tremendous. Did you know that too much complaining has lasting and negative impact on the brain? According to an article I read "Complaining is bad for your Brain"[27], the problem with many complaints today is that they can become a way to vent, as opposed to a way to problem solve. When you stay focused on a complaint, you are empowering negativity and allowing it to expand and take over. Thus, rather than resolving problems and creating change, complaining can become ineffective and create unnecessary stress. The stress caused by complaining can have a lasting and negative impact on the brain. Studies have shown that even a few days of stress damages the neurons in the hippocampus (the part of the brain used for problem solving and cognitive functioning) and impairs its ability to create new neurons. Over time, this can result in the hippocampus shrinking, which can cause a decline in cognitive functions such as memory and the ability to adapt to new situations. A study by Hampel and colleagues (2008) has also found that the hippocampus is one of the first regions of the brain to suffer damage in those with Alzheimer's disease. Your brain's hippocampus is impaired by your own complaining, but how is it affected by listening to the complaining of others? Complaining can be compared to smoking. For the reason that you do not have to be the one complaining about it to affect your health. Listening to other people complaining can have the same negative impact on the brain, as it does when you are the one doing the complaining.[28]

As Joyce Meyer says, "Complain and remain. Praise and be raised." You decide. Which one

> Complain and remain. Praise and be raised.

is it going to be? Complain or Praise? Remember what happened to the people who were delivered from Egypt? Did they make it to the promise land, or did they die in the desert? That's right. They all died with the exception of two, who refuse to join to the complaining murmuring clan. Because of their constant grumbling, murmuring and complaints they died in the in-between process. Don't get caught up with the urge to complain. Paul encourages us to give thanks in everything (1 Thessalonians 5:18). What is everything? Simple, in the good times as much in the bad times.

When Paul and Silas decide to praise, they weren't thinking about themselves. They had all those other prisoners in mind. They took advantage of the opportunity to witness through songs and praises. Praise gets our focus off ourselves and back on God. In return, not only are our spirits refreshed and renewed, but it paves the way for God's power to be displayed and miracles to happen. Little did they know that their praise, and songs would cause such explosion. Had they known that God would respond to their midnight hour praise, they would have started church service earlier. But God showed up and as always showed off. Scriptures tell us that as a result of their praises an earthquake occurred breaking both the chains and shackles, as well as opening the cell doors.

Listen, when God does something, he will not do it halfway. He is going to make sure that you know he was in town. He did not just break the chains, he opened the door that had been shut, locked and tightly sealed. The praise of two physically wounded man, brought about deliverance and salvation that night. Sometimes the things we go through has nothing to do with us and everything with those around us. We are the portals, the vessels, and channel in which God wants to use for others to know of Him and come to Him. Why then are you still holding back your praise? Do you know that your family, children, neighbors, friends, and coworkers are waiting on you?

I remember the first time I spoke about how my marriage had been hit by a storm, that left us broken and heading into separate directions. I really didn't plan to speak about this on that particular day, but something inside me kept nudging at my heart to do so. As I began to speak, I couldn't help but notice that my eyes had become fixed on a particular young lady. There really wasn't anything unusual about her, but it was as if she was the only one in the room who I was speaking to. Little did I know that she would benefit from what for me was the worst nine months of my life. My testimony was her light at the end of the tunnel, was the ray of hope that if God had done with me, if definitely could with her. Therefore, stop complaining about what you don't have, or who wronged you or whatever the issue may be in your life right now. Embrace it. Nothing happens by chance. There is a reason for your suffering, pain, tribulation, storm. Open your mouth and release a sound of praise. You'll be surprised on what will take place.

Still not convinced about this praise thing? Judah, who was Leah's fourth son with Jacob, became the leader in praise. God bypassed the normal line of succession and chose Judah to be the one to represent Jacob's son and his people. Take a look at the following two stories recorded in The Bible:

> Now after the death of Joshua it came to pass, that the children of Israel asked the Lord, saying, who shall go up for us against the Canaanites first, to fight against them? And the Lord said, Judah shall go up: behold, I have delivered the land into his hand. –Judges 1:1-2

> And when they began to sing and to praise, the Lord set ambushments against the children of Ammon, Moab, and mount Seir, which were come against Judah; and they were smitten. –2 Chronicles 20:22

The supernatural power of praise opened the heavenlies and God stepped into an impossible situation and God's people didn't have to lift a finger. Think about what God can do with your situation, your constant enemy that lurks around threatening your health, finances, family, and ministry. I encourage you today to allow yourself to release a shout of praise that has been locked up inside you. Trust me, you will not regret it. When we open our mouths and praise

God, it invites the presence of God and causes the enemy to flee. Praise is a powerful weapon.

It is so powerful, that the enemy seeks to silence you in the midst of your pain, your crisis and situation. He would rather see you focus on the situation at hand than the supernatural power that lays within your praise. Never leave home without it. As we all know, once we conceive that baby is not born overnight. It takes time to develop, until the right moment it's ready to come. A Judah praise isn't birth either overnight. This praise separates you and transitions you from one atmosphere to another. It positions you on the path that leads to your destiny.

> Praise is a powerful weapon.

Like Hannah, when she released what she had stored up in her heart at Shiloh—anger, resentment, sadness, bitterness —she came down a different woman and the Lord remembered her (1 Samuel 1:19). You mean that the Lord forgot about Hannah? Absolutely not. If there is someone who doesn't forget about you, is the Lord. He is one that you can count on at all times. He remembered his plan and purpose with her. She was ready to carry out his masterpiece. She was ready to conceive and influence the life of the prophet who would be incubated in her womb. Influence not by complaining but by the power and effect of praise.

She was ready to be more than a mother. Are you ready for the bigger picture in your life?

Scriptures to Discover Your Identity in Christ

THERE IS NOTHING like the word of God to discover who you are. His word will not lie. It is our assurance that we He says shall be and come to pass.

Accepted in Christ

- I am complete in Christ...Colossians 2:10
- I am God's child...John 1:12
- I am justified...Romans 5:1

Secure in Christ

- I am free from any condemning charges against me... Romans 8:33-34
- I am a citizen of heavan... Phillipians 3:20
- I am hidden in Christ...Colossians 3:3

Significant in Christ

- I am seated with Christ in heavenly places...
Ephesians 2:6
- I am God's coworker...2 Corinthians 6:1
- I am a branch of the true vine, a channel of His life...
John 15:1,5

Scriptures for a Weary Soul

But they that wait upon the Lord shall renew their strength; they shall mount up with wings as eagles; they shall run, and not be weary; and they shall walk, and not faint. — **Isaiah 40:31**

Fear thou not; for I am with thee: be not dismayed; for I am thy God: I will strengthen thee; yea, I will help thee; yea, I will uphold thee with the right hand of my righteousness. —**Isaiah 41:10**

And kings shall be thy nursing fathers, and their queens thy nursing mothers: they shall bow down to thee with their face toward the earth, and lick up the dust of thy feet; and thou shalt know that I am the Lord: for they shall not be ashamed that wait for me. —**Isaiah 49:23**

My brethren, count it all joy when ye fall into divers temptations, knowing this, that the trying of your faith worketh patience. But let patience have her perfect work, that ye may be perfect and entire, wanting nothing. If any of you lack wisdom, let him ask of God, that giveth to all men liberally, and upbraideth not; and if shall be given him. —**James 1:2-5**

Come unto me, all ye that labour and are heavy laden, and I will give you rest. —**Matthew 11:28**

These things I have spoken unto you, that in me ye might have peace. In the world ye shall have tribulation: but be of good cheer; I have overcome the world. —**John 16:33**

The Lord will perfect that which concerneth me: thy mercy, O Lord, endureth for ever: forsake not the works of thine own hands. —**Psalm 138:8**

Rejoice in hope; patient in tribulation; continuing instant in prayer; —**Romans 12:12**

And we know that all things work together for good to them that love God, to them who are called according to his purpose. —**Romans 8:28**

And let us not be weary in well doing: for in due season we shall reap, if we faint not. —**Galatians 6:9**

About the Author

Taysha Morales is a mother of three handsome young men and serves in ministry alongside her husband and pastor, Eduardo Morales. Taysha has found a passion and love for the word of God, which she shares with everyone who comes across her path. Among the many hats she wears –*mother, sister, daughter, first lady, preacher, teacher* – she has managed to add one more as an author. As founder of the Women Ministry in 2015 "This is your time," she has reached the hearts of many leading them back to Jesus for healing, deliverance and restoration. She is an empowered woman filled with the wisdom of God, who's had to learn to awaken the warrior in her for such a time as this.

For additional works published by author, please visit Amazon.com and lulu.com.

Endnotes

1   Deleterious: causing harm or damage.

2   Henry Ford Quotes. BrainyQuote.com, BrainyMedia Inc, 2021. https://www.brainyquote.com/quotes/henry_ford_121339, accessed February 8, 2021

3   https://www.google.com/search?q=this+is+my+story+quote&safe=strict&rlz=1C1CHBF_enUS859US859&sxsrf=ALeKk01wm7I5i0C9CU-DcpR-3wLcDc2OYRA:1616096456587&tbm=isch&source=iu&ictx=1&fir=8Lw0JHy0em_DQM%252Cxm3b2Ai4BgQSCM%252C_&vet=1&usg=AI4_-kTLRE4yOw1Nqr6sRptygy3Li5Qm9w&sa=X&ved=2ahUKEwjBmN65zLrvAhVnAp0JHSB-CK0Q9QF6BAgPEAE&biw=1280&bih=578#imgrc=L-VaTqmfCZ1-_YM (accessed March 18, 2021)

4   https://www.google.com/search?q=this+is+my+story+quote&safe=strict&rlz=1C1CHBF_enUS859US859&sxsrf=ALeKk01wm7I5i0C9CU-DcpR-3wLcDc2OYRA:1616096456587&tbm=isch&source=iu&ictx=1&fir=8Lw0JHy0em_DQM%252Cxm3b2Ai4BgQSCM%252C_&vet=1&us

g=AI4_-kTLRE4yOw1Nqr6sRptygy3Li5Qm9w&s
a=X&ved=2ahUKEwjBmN65zLrvAhVnAp0JHSB-
CK0Q9QF6BAgPEAE&biw=1280&bih=578#-
imgrc=D1hrjQRmFDt1iM (accessed March 18, 2021)

5 https://hbr.org/2005/01/whats-your-story (accessed
   February 3, 2021)

6 https://www.vocabulary.com/dictionary/shadow
   (accessed March 29, 2021)

7 http://amazingsciencefactsforkids.blogspot.
   com/2016/10/7-interesting-facts-about-light-and.
   html#:~:text=A%20shadow%20happens%20
   when%20an,side%20for%20a%20little%20while.
   (access March 29, 2021)

8 Michelle McClain-Walters, The Deborah Anointing:
   Embracing the call to be a Woman of Wisdom and
   Discernment (Lake Mary, FL: Charisma House, 2015)

9 Melodic: of, having, or producing melody; pleas-
   ant-sounding; melodious.

10 https://www.psychologytoday.com/us/blog/test-
   case/201204/so-whats-your-story (accessed on
   February 5, 2021)

11 Boisterous: rough and noisy; noisily jolly or rowdy;
   clamorous; unrestrained:

12 Five out the seven were Leah's biological children – Ruben, Simeon, Judah, Issachar and Zabulun. The other two were from her handmaid Zilpah – Gad and Asher.

13 https://www.azquotes.com/quotes/topics/lost-and-found.html (accessed May 7, 2021)

14 https://www.ncfgiving.com/stories/2-types-of-weary/ (accessed February 10, 2021)

15 https://www.chaimbentorah.com/2018/01/word-study-weary/ (accessed February 10, 2021)

16 https://www.etymonline.com/word/process (accessed February 12, 2021)

17 https://thelife.com/devotionals/an-expected-end (accessed on February 11, 2021)

18 Biologydictionary.net Editors. "Metamorphosis." Biology Dictionary, Biologydictionary.net, 04 Jul. 2017, https://biologydictionary.net/metamorphosis/. (accessed February 15, 2021)

19 https://www.natgeokids.com/uk/discover/animals/insects/butterfly-life-cycle/ (accessed February 16, 2021)

20 https://bestquotehd.blogspot.com/2020/10/15-inspirational-quotes-and-home.html (accessed May 7, 2021)

21 https://www.google.com/search?q=healing+doesn%27t+mean+the+damage&safe=strict&rlz=1C1CHBF_enUS859US859&sxsrf=ALeKk031-60G5k-9WwFW0FPGmw8cBIK-WrTQ:1616176312865&tbm=isch&source=iu&ictx=1&fir=Bqtolid1zJWE3M%252C1n3I_KcqaLzQFM%252C_&vet=1&usg=AI4_-kR255P_vTrSAXcAR-6LtXt19H96HA&sa=X&ved=2ahUKEwib6Jb49bzvAhWaHM0KHXccCwMQ9QF-6BAgSEAE&biw=1920&bih=937&dpr=1#imgrc=VRtf_m_J2Z69sM (accessed March 19, 2021)

22 https://www.merriam-webster.com/dictionary/sickness (accessed March 16, 2021)

23 https://static1.squarespace.com/static/56c-b43860442628a65205b5d/t/57f7f9d8b8a79bc-648bcd3d1/1475869155472/Pick+Up+Your+Matt.pdf (March 1, 2021)

24 https://www.google.com/search?q=when+you+enter+god%27s+presence+with+praise&safe=strict&rlz=1C-1CHBF_enUS859US859&sxsrf=ALeKk01iQR9gMWErPaJNW2iHu8R0FwYcYw:1615598991758&tbm=isch&source=iu&ictx-

= 1 & fir = Wtv QjzyJiUk-lM%252CzvlXXgxfB-
fORCM%252C_&vet=1&usg=AI4_-kTPPpG-
PiZDNVrZO7ytZ4nNM4BjXVA&sa=X&ved=2a-
hUKEwiIy4Kgj6zvAhXMW80KHYEvBLMQ9QF-
6BAgDEAE&biw=1920&bih=937#imgrc=4rkw-
Cz2j5VULRM (accessed March 12, 2021)

25 https://www.peterwade.com/law-of-first-men-
tion/?v=7516fd43adaa (accessed March 14, 2021)

26 https://www.lexico.com/definition/connection
(accessed March 14, 2021)

27 https://m1psychology.com/complaining-is-bad-for-
your-brain/#:~:text=The%20stress%20caused%20
by%20complaining,ability%20to%20create%20
new%20neurons. (accessed March 16, 2021)

28 https://m1psychology.com/complaining-is-bad-for-
your-brain/ (accessed March 16, 2021)

29 https://www.google.com/search?q=who+am+i
+in+christ&safe=strict&rlz=1C1CHBF_enU-
S859US859&sxsrf=ALeKk02zsrjgJkHW7hkWfI-
jqDci7tbfkrA:1620231634661&source=lnms&tb-
m=isch&sa=X&ved=2ahUKEwiPn6aY-bLwA
h W K b s 0 K H e a S D o g Q _
A U o A X o E C A E Q A w & b i w = 1 9 2 0 & b i h
=937#imgrc=xsODuSEDhKzh1M (accessed May
5, 2021)

9 781662 8199